Risk and Management Accounting: Best Practice Guidelines for Enterprise-wide Internal Control Procedures

Paul M Collier
Anthony J Berry
Gary T Burke

AMSTERDAM • BOSTON • HEIDELBERG • LONDON • NEW YORK • OXFORD
PARIS • SAN DIEGO • SAN FRANCISCO • SINGAPORE • SYDNEY • TOKYO

CIMA Publishing is an imprint of Elsevier

CIMA Publishing is an imprint of Elsevier
Linacre House, Jordan Hill, Oxford OX2 8DP
30 Corporate Drive, Suite 400, Burlington, MA 01803, USA

First edition 2007

1005072882

British Library Cataloguing in Publication Data
A catalogue record for this book is available from the British Library

Library of Congress Cataloguing in Publication Data
A catalogue record for this book is available from the Library of Congress

ISBN-13: 978-0-7506-8040-0
ISBN-10: 0-7506-8040-7

For information on all Butterworth-Heinemann publications
visit our web site at http://books.elsevier.com

Printed and bound in Great Britain

07 08 09 10   10 9 8 7 6 5 4 3 2 1

Working together to grow
libraries in developing countries

www.elsevier.com | www.bookaid.org | www.sabre.org

ELSEVIER   BOOK AID
International   Sabre Foundation

Contents

Contents

vii

About the Authors

Dr Paul M Collier was senior lecturer in management accounting at Aston Business School but is now at the Department of Accounting and Finance, Monash University in Melbourne, Australia. Before becoming an academic, Paul held a number of senior financial and general management positions in Australia and the UK.

Professor Anthony J Berry is Professor in the Business School at Manchester Metropolitan University. After ten years in the UK and US aircraft industries he became a faculty member of the Manchester Business School. He was later Director of the Management Research Institute at Sheffield Hallam University. His research interests include management control, risk, consultancy and leadership. He has published extensively in UK and international journals.

Gary T Burke worked as the Research Assistant on the CIMA-funded risk management project, while studying for his part-time MBA. He has worked as a financial analyst for a number of large UK PLCs and has managed the Management Development Programme at Aston University. He is currently undertaking an ESRC-sponsored PhD at Aston University exploring public-private partnerships.

Acknowledgements

The authors gratefully thank CIMA for providing research funds that enabled the case studies, survey and analysis described in this report to be carried out. We are also grateful for the comments of two anonymous reviewers on an earlier version of this report.

Acknowledgements

xi

List of Figures

List of Tables

Executive Summary

Introduction

This book presents the findings from two research projects on risk funded by grants provided by CIMA. The first grant was for a pilot study comprising four mini-case studies. Our major focus in that study was on how risk impacted upon budgeting. The second grant was for a comprehensive survey and analysis of risk management in organisations and, in particular, how risk management impacted on both internal controls and on the role of the management account- ant. Following the statistical analysis of the survey, interviews were conducted with survey respondents and risk management profes- sionals in order to help us explain our findings. This report there- fore provides the results of these three phases of our research.

The book contains:

A review of the practitioner and academic literature as it affects governance, risk management and management accounting.

- ◆ The four exploratory case studies.
- ◆ A comprehensive description of the survey design and results.
- ◆ Excerpts from the interview data in relation to the survey results.
- ◆ A summary of the research findings.
- ◆ Implications for best practice.

Risk and risk management

Risk has traditionally been defined in terms of the possibility of danger, loss, injury or other adverse consequences. In accounting and finance, risk is considered in terms of decision trees, probabil- ity distributions, cost-volume-profit analysis, discounted cash flow, capital assets pricing models and hedging techniques, etc.

Risk management is the process by which organisations methodi- cally address the risks attaching to their activities in pursuit of organisational objectives and across the portfolio of all their activ- ities. Effective risk management involves risk assessment, risk eval- uation, risk treatment, and risk reporting. The focus of good risk management is the identification and treatment of those risks in accordance with the organisation's risk appetite. The enterprise risk management approach is intended to align risk management with business strategy and embed a risk management culture into business operations.

The Committee of Sponsoring Organisations of the Treadway Commission (COSO) (2004) model of internal control comprises eight components:

1. The internal environment sets the basis for how risk is viewed and the organisational appetite for risk.
2. Organisational objectives must be consistent with risk appetite.
3. Events affecting achievement of objectives must be identified, distinguishing between risks and opportunities.
4. Risk assessment involves the analysis of risks into their likelihood and impact in order to determine how they should be managed.
5. Management then selects risk responses in terms of how risks may be mitigated, transferred or held.
6. Control activities in the form of policies and procedures ensure that risk responses are carried out effectively.
7. Information needs to be captured and communicated as the basis for risk management.
8. The enterprise risk management system should be regularly monitored and evaluated.

(Source: Committee of Sponsoring Organisations of the Treadway Commission (COSO), 2004) *Enterprise Risk Management – Integrated Framework.*

Case study findings: process and content of budgeting

The purpose of the exploratory case studies was to understand the relationship between risk and budgeting. This involved consideration of how risk was enacted in budgeting and how managerial perceptions of risk influenced the process and content of budgets. The findings from the four case studies reveal differences based on the contexts of unique circumstances, histories and technologies of the organisations. The four cases illustrated how the different social constructions of participants in the budgeting process influenced the domains – or alternative lenses – through which the process of budgeting took place and how the content of the budget was determined.

Four domains of risk were observed, reflecting the different social constructions of participants – financial, operational, political and personal. The *process* of budgeting in all four cases was characterised as risk considered, in which a top-down budgeting process reflected negotiated targets. By contrast, the *content* of budget documents was risk excluded, being based on a set of single-point estimates, in which all of the significant risks were excluded from the budget itself. The separation of budgeting and risk management has significant consequences for the management of risk as the process of budgeting needs to be considered separately from the content of budget documents.

Objective and subjective risk

Despite the traditional accounting and finance emphasis, many risks are not objectively identifiable and measurable but are subjective and qualitative. For example, the risks of litigation, economic downturns, loss of key employees, natural disasters, and loss of reputation are all subjective judgements. Risk is, therefore, to a considerable extent, 'socially constructed' and responses to risk reflect that social construction.

There is an important distinction between objective, measurable risk and subjective, perceived risk. Risk can be thought about by reference to the existence of internal or external events, information about those events (i.e. their visibility), managerial perception about events and information (i.e. how they are perceived), and how organisations establish tacit/informal or explicit/formal ways of dealing with risk.

Adams (1995) has shown that everyone has a propensity to take risks, but this propensity to take risks varies from person to person, being influenced by the potential rewards of risk taking and perceptions of risk, which are influenced by experience of 'accidents'. Hence, individual risk taking represents a balance between perceptions of risk and the propensity to take risks.

Prior research shows that we know little about how managers consider risks but managers do take risks, based on risk preferences at individual and organisational levels. Some of these risk preferences vary with national cultures while others are individual traits. Risk perception is a cultural process, with each culture each set of shared values and supporting social institutions being biased toward highlighting certain risks and downplaying others. We found that this socially constructed view of risk was a better reflection of organisational risk management than rational modelling approaches typified by textbooks and professional training as it reflected the subjectivity of risk perceptions and preferences, cultural constraints and individual traits. The four 'ideal types' developed by Adams (1995) and adapted in the full report as risk stance – risk sceptical (or fatalists), hierarchists, individualists, and risk aware (or egalitarians) – was helpful in our research in understanding individual and organisational risk management practices. Our survey found that the risk stance of managers did influence the risk management practices in use.

Risk management survey

Following the case studies, it was decided to undertake a survey of organisations in the UK to examine risk management practices and the role of management accountants in risk management. The relationships we conjectured during our research design are shown in Figure S.1.

Figure S.1 Conjectured relationships in our study

Subsequently, we conducted a survey of CIMA members, finance directors of FTSE listed companies and chief executives of SMEs and analysed 333 usable responses, a response rate of 11 per cent. We subsequently interviewed a number of respondents to aid our interpretation of the survey analysis.

Risk management practices

We found that risk management systems appeared to improve the organisational capacity to process information, both through vertical information systems but also through the role of risk managers, whose role was a cross-functional one, supporting the distinction made between event-uncertainty, commonly viewed as risk, and information-uncertainty (Galbraith, 1977: p.4).

The survey found that the methods for risk management that were in highest use were the more subjective ones (particularly experience), with quantitative methods used least of all. These results suggested a heuristic method of risk management is at work in contrast to the systems-based approach that is associated with risk management in much professional training and in the professional literature. The survey responses implied that traditional methods of managing risk through transfer (insurance, hedging, etc.) were still seen as more effective than more proactive risk management processes. Risk was seen on an individual level as much about achieving positive consequences as avoiding negative ones. However, organisational risk management was reported to be more about avoiding negative consequences.

In terms of methods of risk management, our interviewees advised us that 'keeping things simple' was best, although more sophisticated techniques were more likely to be used at lower organisational levels. This was largely because business was so complex and supposedly 'objective' methods may not be as reliable as they are sometimes perceived to be.

The trends in risk management were reported to have shifted from being considered tacitly to being considered more formally and the survey results reflected the respondents' expectation that this trend will shift markedly to a more holistic approach with risk management being used to aid decision-making. Interviewees provided examples of the beginning of a shift to a more proactive stance towards risk management where this was seen to deliver business benefits. There was a strong emphasis from our interviewees that this shift was likely to increase with a move away from the 'tick box' approach. It was accepted by our interviewees that there was a need culturally to embed risk into organisations as a taken-for-granted practice.

Costs and benefits of risk management

Risk management may be seen largely as a compliance exercise. However, half of the respondents reported that the benefits exceeded the costs, with 40 per cent reporting that benefits and costs were neutral. Although this was a subjective judgement, the Vice President of a European federation of risk management associations summed up the benefits as:

> An organisation that doesn't issue profit warnings, doesn't have major unjustified exceptional costs on its annual accounts because they thought about things in advance. They have managed acquisitions and mergers proactively to ensure that they have met their targets and objectives and haven't impaired the goodwill or asset values. These are some of the things you might see. A profitable and successful company, excellent reputation, corporate social responsibility – you wouldn't see them being fingered as people who are exploiting the third world, child labour, etc. – all those things sort of come out of it. They have got their supply chain issues sorted out. I guess out in the City, analysts are comfortable with what they are hearing and probably their estimates are pretty close to what the organisation achieves. Good credit rating, because they can see that they are good value and their ratios are all good.

Governance and the drivers of risk management

The *Combined Code on Corporate Governance* (Financial Reporting Council, 2003) is an important motivator for risk management and internal control practices, requiring Boards to maintain a sound system of internal control to safeguard shareholders' investment and the company's assets. Internal control is the whole system of internal controls, financial and otherwise, established in order to provide reasonable assurance of effective and efficient operation, internal financial control, and compliance with laws and regulations. However, as profits are, in part, the reward for successful risk taking in business then the purpose of internal control is to help manage and control risk appropriately rather than to eliminate it.

Given the significant public visibility of corporate governance requirements, our survey findings suggested that risk management may be seen largely as a compliance exercise. Management action to decrease the likelihood of risk was given the highest ranking by respondents, rather than action to achieve organisational objectives. Risk still appears to be dominated by downside concerns and risk transfer through hedging and insurance remains dominant over proactive risk management practices.

Contrary to expectations that risk management practices vary between organisations as a result of their size or industry sector, there was little evidence of any contingent explanations for risk management based on either size or business sector. Similarly, if somewhat surprisingly, respondents' perceptions of the environmental uncertainty and risk facing their organisations did not appear to influence basic risk management practices in those organisations.

The survey results suggested that risk management was driven by an institutional response to calls for improved corporate governance which may reflect both protection and economic opportunity. The external drivers of risk management practices were observed to be external stakeholders and the demands of regulators and legislation, enacted through boards of directors which were likely to exert influence over the policies and methods adopted for risk management.

Financial market risk

In relation to financial market risk, the implication of our regression analysis is that the 'risk aware' stance, in attending to both protection and to opportunity, does create organisations to which the capital markets award a lower *beta*, and hence a higher value. This led us to infer that the requirements of corporate governance do not necessarily have to work in opposition to economic ratio-nales of risk as opportunity and adventure. However, given the small samples, this observation is indicative only and would need to be replicated on a larger scale.

Framework for risk management

Our survey results, amplified by our interview data, enabled us to put forward a framework for risk management. This framework reflects the primary research findings, in particular that:

◆ There are many external drivers to risk management, not only regulatory, but that these are enacted by or through the board of directors.
◆ Other than organisation size, there appears to be no correlation between environmental uncertainty or competitive factors and risk management practices.
◆ Risk propensity was not as important as risk stance.
◆ Risk management practices exist along a continuum of heuristic to systematic but, at corporate level, the heuristic methods dominate.
◆ Risk management practices are believed by respondents to move along a life cycle from heuristic to systems dependent to culturally embedded.
◆ The involvement of accountants in risk management was marginal.
◆ Risk management was perceived to improve organisational performance and there is indication that a risk aware stance could be related to a lower capital market risk profile.

The framework, in conjunction with that developed by Solomon et al. (2000) presents a useful model for understanding how risk management practices are introduced and develop over time.

Risk and management accountants

Management accountants, whose professional training included the analysis of information and systems, performance and strategic management, can have a significant role to play in developing and implementing risk management and internal control systems within their organisations (Chartered Institute of Management Accountants, 2002).

These research results have some significant implications for the role of accountants. The responses reveal that line managers were mostly concerned with identifying risk, analysing and reporting on risk. Finance directors had a major role in analysing and assessing, and reporting and monitoring risk. Deciding on risk management action was predominantly the concern of the chief executive and the board. The finance director was identified with more aspects of risk management than any other role, suggesting that they probably have a pivotal role in risk management.

The changing role of management accountants is an important factor in establishing the context for their role in risk management and wider views of management control. Perhaps reinforcing traditional stereotypes, CIMA respondents were more risk-concerned than the other respondent groups in relation to their organisations, despite having a lower perception of the competitive intensity and uncertainty in their industry/sector.

The reliance on formal accounting-based controls was also called into question. Importantly, CIMA respondents were less confident in the formal control systems that existed in their organisations, suggesting that the professional knowledge of accountants accommodates an understanding of the limits of accounting information, a knowledge not shared by non-accountants.

Further, management accountants in the overwhelming majority of organisations were being marginalised in relation to risk management. While CIMA respondents consider that management accountants should have more involvement in risk management, this was not a view shared by other respondents.

Interviewees saw the skill set of management accountants as not being appropriate to a wider involvement in risk management, although their analytic and modelling skills were essential in a supporting role. The distinction between task-oriented management accountants and strategic finance directors was reinforced in our interviews.

Best practice implications

Based on our research, our report highlights some fundamental best practice implications for risk management:

◆ taking a broader opportunistic approach to risk management, based on a risk/return trade-off, rather than a purely defensive or protective stance
◆ using appropriate and effective tools, but these tools should be supplemented by experience, intuition and judgement
◆ a deliberately proactive stance towards risk management, rather than an excessive reliance on traditional techniques, except to the extent that these techniques remain useful
◆ emphasising the importance of culturally embedding risk awareness in organisations
◆ training users of financial information in the limitations of that information.

There are further best practice implications for CIMA and its members:

◆ The role of management accountants needs to shift towards a more strategic and value adding role which, by definition, includes a consideration of risk, if management accountants are not to be marginalised in risk management processes.
◆ CIMA members may have to reach finance director positions before they can contribute more significantly to risk management, but clearly they should be educated to be able to fulfil that function.

Introduction

This book presents the findings from two research projects on risk funded by grants provided by CIMA. The first grant was for a pilot study comprising four mini-case studies. Our major focus in that study was on how risk impacted upon budgeting. The second grant was for a comprehensive survey and analysis of risk management in organisations and, in particular, how risk management impacted on both internal controls and on the role of the management accountant. Following the statistical analysis of the survey, interviews were conducted with survey respondents and risk management professionals in order to help us explain our findings. This book therefore provides the results of these three phases of our research.

Chapter 1 provides a review of the practitioner and academic literature as it affects governance, risk management and management accounting. This chapter contains a summary of the literature on risk as it affects management control and the role of the management accountant. First, the major influence of corporate governance requirements on risk management is reviewed. Then risk definitions are examined and set in the context of the practitioner literature on risk management. Second, academic notions of risk as it affects managers, internal control and the role of the accountant are examined.

Chapter 2 describes the four exploratory case studies. The purpose of the exploratory case studies was to understand the relationship between risk and budgeting. This involved consideration of how risk was enacted in budgeting and how managerial perceptions of risk influenced the process and content of budgets. *Risk modelled* budgeting was conjectured as a descriptive model of the environment–organisation interface through input–output modelling which assumes knowledge of the means–ends transformation process. A budgetary system designed within an implicit protective boundary where risk is explicitly excluded from the budgetary system and is managed in some other domain was proposed as a *risk excluded* form of budget. Where organisations give attention to environmental influences, while simultaneously creating a protective boundary, albeit in different elements of the budgetary system, a *risk considered* form of budgeting was conjectured.

Following the case studies, it was decided to undertake a survey of organisations in the UK to examine risk management practices and the role of management accountants in risk management. Chapter 3 provides a comprehensive description of the survey design, the survey instrument, the method of analysis and the results of that analysis.

To help us to interpret some of the findings in the analysis of our survey results, we conducted interviews with 14 members of organisations, who had indicated in their survey questionnaires that they were prepared to be interviewed. Ten were interviewed face to face and four by telephone. The interviews were based on semi-structured, open questions in order not to lead the respondents. Transcripts of the interviews were made for later analysis. This chapter is based upon excerpts from these interviews, in order to explore the key issues emerging from the survey. Chapter 4 provides excerpts from our interview data in relation to our survey results.

The research findings are summarized in Chapter 5 and Chapter 6 contains implications for best practice.

Governance, risk and control

Introduction

This chapter contains a summary of the literature on risk as it affects management control and the role of the management accountant. First, the major influence of corporate governance requirements on risk management is reviewed. Then risk definitions are examined and set in the context of the practitioner literature on risk management. Second, academic notions of risk as it affects managers, internal control and the role of the accountant are examined.

Corporate governance

Corporate governance is the system by which companies are directed and controlled. Boards of directors are responsible for the governance of their companies. The shareholders' role in governance is to appoint the directors and the auditors and to satisfy themselves that an appropriate governance structure is in place. The responsibilities of the board include setting the company's strategic aims, providing the leadership to put them into effect, supervising the management of the business and reporting to shareholders on their stewardship. The board's actions are subject to laws, regulations and the shareholders in general meeting (CIMA *Official Terminology*).

Even before the spate of corporate governance reports, culminating in the *Combined Code on Corporate Governance* (Financial Reporting Council, 2003), a growing number of institutional investors were starting to encourage greater disclosure of governance processes and emphasising the quality and sustainability of earnings, rather than short-term profits alone. For example, a survey published by KPMG in 2002 (KPMG, 2003) reported that 80 per cent of fund managers would pay more for the shares of a demonstrably well-governed company, with the average premium being 11 per cent. Research by management consultants McKinsey (McKinsey & Co, 2006) has also shown that an overwhelming majority of institutional investors are prepared to pay a significant premium for companies exhibiting high standards of corporate governance.

The media have also increased their reporting of governance practices. The high-profile failures of companies, notably the press coverage given to Enron and WorldCom, brought corporate governance to worldwide attention. The September 11 (2001) attacks in the USA also resulted in an increase in attention to risk.

This increased attention to corporate governance has been a global one. Policy concern with corporate governance has been driven in recent years by a series of corporate scandals and failures in a number of countries, not just due to cyclical events but also to systemic weaknesses. Major corporate collapses have been a feature of recent business history in the UK and elsewhere. Among these have been:

◆ In the UK, high-profile failures have occurred in the Maxwell publishing group, Bank of Commerce & Credit International (BCCI), Asil Nadir's Polly Peck, and Marconi.
◆ In Italy, there has been Pasminco, and in Australia the insurer HIH, Ansett Airlines, and OneTel.
◆ Most high profile has been the corporate collapses in the USA: Enron, WorldCom, and Tyco.

Corporate governance considerations emerged in the USA in the Treadway Commission's Report on *Fraudulent Financial Reporting* in 1987 (Treadway Commission, 1987), which was later reinforced by the Securities and Exchange Commission in its listing requirements. A subgroup of the Treadway Commission, the Committee of Sponsoring Organisations (COSO) developed *Internal Control – Integrated Framework* in 1992 (Committee of Sponsoring Organisations of the Treadway Commission, 1992) and, in 2003, a report was published on *Enterprise Risk Management* (Committee of Sponsoring Organisations of the Treadway Commission, 2003) which was updated in 2004 (Committee of Sponsoring Organisations of the Treadway Commission, 2004).

The introduction of the US Sarbanes-Oxley Act in 2002 was the legislative response in the USA to the financial and accounting scandals of Enron and WorldCom and the misconduct at the accounting firm Arthur Andersen. Its main aim was to deal with core issues of transparency, integrity and oversight of financial markets.

The emergence of corporate governance as a problem can be traced to enforcement exercises in relation to past misdeeds, changing financial markets, including the rapid rise of institutional investors and their increasing desire to be more active investors, and the increasing dependence of an ageing population on pensions and savings which have been affected by declining confidence in stock markets.

In the UK, a series of reports has had a marked influence on the development of corporate governance. The first report, by Sir Adrian Cadbury, followed corporate failures in Polly Peck, BCCI and pension funds in the Maxwell Group. The Cadbury Report (Cadbury Code, 1992) was in relation to *Financial Aspects of Corporate Governance.* The Greenbury report on directors' remuneration was published in 1995 (Greenbury, 1995). The Hampel report, published in 1998 (Committee on Corporate Governance, 1988), reviewed the implementation of the Cadbury Code. The *Corporate Governance Combined Code,* published in 1998 (Financial Reporting Council, 2003), incorporated the recommendations of the Cadbury, Greenbury and Hampel Committees. This was superseded by the *Combined Code on Corporate Governance* (Financial Reporting Council, 2003) which incorporated the Turnbull Guidance on internal control (Institute of Chartered Accountants in England & Wales, 1999), the Higgs report on the role of non-executive directors and the Smith report on the role of audit committees, both published in 2003 (Higgs, 2003; Smith, 2003).

In 2003, the publication by CIMA (2003) of *Enterprise Governance: Getting the Balance Right*, emphasised the importance of a dual concern with conformance and performance. Conformance was related to issues of accountability and assurance, driven by corporate governance requirements. Performance was concerned with resource utilisation and value creation. CIMA's enterprise governance framework argued the need to balance conformance requirements with the need to deliver long-term performance to achieve strategic success.

Risk

Risk is typically defined in terms of the possibility of danger, loss, injury or other adverse consequences. The distinction between risk and uncertainty is typically made in accounting and finance texts and dates back to Knight's classic work *Risk, uncertainty and profit*, published in 1921 (Knight, 1921). According to Knight, risk was a state of not knowing what future events will happen, but having the ability to estimate the odds, while uncertainty was a state of not knowing the odds. While the first was calculable, the second was not and any estimates were subjective. The *Risk Management Standard* (Institute of Risk Management, 2002) defined risk as the combination of the probability of an event and its consequences, with risk management being concerned with both positive and negative aspects of risk.

The discipline of risk management has emerged, initially from insurance, but subsequently from many fields including health and safety, environmental pollution, crisis management, business continuity, project risk, and reputation risk. Professional bodies, consulting firms and academics have produced many hundreds of publications on risk management during the last decade.

The accounting literature, as it is reflected in textbooks, has addressed risk from a narrow perspective. Accounting texts, so far as they discuss risk, do so in terms of decision trees, probability distributions, cost-volume-profit analysis, discounted cash flow etc. Finance texts are typically concerned with portfolios, capital assets pricing models and hedging techniques to reduce the risks of currency and interest rate exposure. However, there are three limitations in these narrow perspectives:

◆ the usefulness (or value) of quantification techniques for measuring risk probabilistically was recognised in the 1930s as being questionable (McGoun, 1995), although this has been forgotten
◆ there has been a reduction of human agency to irrelevance
◆ risk has traditionally been viewed as negative, despite the well accepted idea of a risk/return trade-off.

The International Federation of Accountants (IFAC, 1999) published an important study on *Enhancing Shareholder Wealth by Better Managing Business Risk*. The IFAC report defined risks as uncertain future events that could influence the achievement of the organisation's strategic, operational and financial objectives. The IFAC report shifted the focus of risk from a negative concept of hazard to a positive interpretation that managing risk is an integral part of generating sustainable shareholder value. The report argued that business risk management establishes, calibrates and realigns the relationship between risk, growth and return.

Similarly, the Turnbull Report (Institute of Chartered Accountants in England & Wales, 1999), now part of the *Combined Code on Corporate Governance*, defined risk as any event that might affect a listed company's performance, including environmental, ethical and social risks.

Risks can be classified in a number of ways. One common distinction is:

◆ Business or operational risk: relating to the activities carried out within an organisation
◆ Financial risk: relating to the financial operation of a business
◆ Environmental risk: relating to changes in the political, economic, social and financial environment
◆ Reputation risk: caused by failing to address some other risk.

The Institute of Risk Management (2002) *Risk Management Standard* categorised risk in terms of financial, strategic, operational and hazard. Some of these risks are driven by external factors (competition, interest rates, regulations, natural events) and some are driven by internal factors (research and development, cash flow, information systems, etc.). Some risks have both external and internal drivers (e.g. employees, supply chains, products and services, and merger and acquisitions).

Building on these distinctions, risk can be thought about by reference to:

◆ the existence of internal or external events
◆ information about those events (i.e. their visibility)
◆ managerial perception about events and information (i.e. how they are perceived)
◆ how organisations establish tacit/informal or explicit/formal ways of dealing with risk.

Clearly, risk can be understood in two basic ways – as potential loss or potential gain. Risk as loss is what managers most often mean when they talk about risk, referring mainly to events with negative consequences. Managing risk in this context means seeking to reduce the probability of the negative event (the downside) without undue cost. Risk as hazard is typically a concern of those responsible for conformance: financial controllers, internal auditors and insurance specialists. Managing risk in this context means reducing the variance between anticipated and actual outcomes. In conditions of uncertainty, chief financial officers and line managers responsible for operations are unable to assess the potential loss or the consequences of their actions.

Risk as opportunity for potential gain accepts that there is a relationship between risk and return. Managing risk in this context means using techniques to maximise the gain while minimising the downside. Shareholders expect boards to achieve a higher return than is possible from risk-free investments such as government securities, and expect boards to be entrepreneurial in taking risks within the accepted risk profile of the organisation.

There is a natural progression in managing risk:

♦ from managing the risk associated with compliance and prevention (the downside)
♦ through managing to minimise the risks of uncertainty in respect of operating performance
♦ to moving to the higher level of managing opportunity risks (the upside) which need to be taken in order to increase and sustain shareholder value.

Organising for uncertainty

The distinction between risk and uncertainty made by Knight to some extent is reflected in the later work of Galbraith who differentiated event uncertainty, commonly viewed as risk, from information uncertainty. The distinction is important, not least because an organisation has little or no control over external events (merely its response to those events). Galbraith defined information uncertainty as the difference between the amount of information required to perform a task and the amount of information already possessed by the organisation. Uncertainty limits the ability of the organisation to make decisions in advance. Galbraith (1977: p.4) argued that:

> the greater the uncertainty of the task, the greater the amount of information that has to be processed between decision makers during its execution.

Galbraith (1974) observed that as task uncertainty increases, the number of exceptions to expectations increases until the hierarchy becomes overloaded. He argued that the success of goal setting, hierarchy and rules depended upon the combination of the frequency of exceptions and the capacity of the hierarchy to handle those exceptions. As uncertainty increased, Galbraith proposed four organisational design strategies:

1. The creation of slack resources minimises exceptions by relaxing budget targets, creating longer delivery lead times and 'buffer' inventories.
2. The creation of self-contained tasks can change the division of labour by allocating resources to an output-focused product group structure instead of a skills-based functional structure. The creation of slack resources and self-contained tasks were strategies that reduced the need for information processing because of lower performance standards, because fewer exceptions were likely to occur and fewer factors would impact on the interdependence between business units.
3. Investing in vertical information systems permits the processing of information as a result of task performance, without overloading the managerial hierarchy. Galbraith argued that unanticipated events created exceptions that incrementally updated the plan, but which, in sufficient quantity, lead to a new plan. This was the path chosen by most risk management advisors and reports.
4. Creating lateral relations might shift decision-making to the location of information, without creating self-contained groups. These relations could be achieved through direct contact between managers, through liaison roles, task forces, teams, and integrating roles. Investing in vertical information systems or creating lateral relations were strategies that increased the organisational capacity to process information.

The effect of a combination of these four design strategies (the creation of slack resources, self-contained tasks, vertical information systems and lateral relations) is to reduce the number of exceptions referred upward in the organisational hierarchy. If one of these design strategies is not chosen, Galbraith argued that performance standards will automatically fall.

Galbraith's ideas are relevant to an understanding of managing risk through control procedures and will provide a point of reference later in this report.

Risk management

Risk management has been defined as the process of understanding and managing the risks that the organisation is inevitably subject to in attempting to achieve its corporate objectives (CIMA *Official Terminology*).

The Institute of Risk Management provided a more detailed definition of risk management as:

> the process by which organisations methodically address the risks attaching to their activities with the goal of achieving sustained benefit within each activity and across the portfolio of all activities.

The focus of good risk management is the identification and treatment of these risks. Its objective is to add maximum sustainable value to all the activities of the organisation. It marshalls the understanding of the potential upside and downside of all those factors which could affect the organisation. It increases the probability of success, and reduces both the probability of failure and the uncertainty of achieving the organisation's overall objectives.

The Institute of Risk Management (2002) developed a *Risk Management Standard,* which contains several elements:

◆ risk assessment
◆ risk evaluation
◆ risk treatment
◆ risk reporting.

Risk assessment comprises the analysis and evaluation of risk through processes of identification, description and estimation. The purpose of risk assessment is to undertake risk evaluation. Risk evaluation is used to make decisions about the significance of risks to the organisation and whether each specific risk should be accepted or treated. Examples of identifying risk are shown in Box 1.1. Various methods may be used to assess the severity of each risk once they are identified, as Box 1.2 shows.

Although many of these methods provide a formal structure for estimating risk, they assume simple linear cause – effect relationships rather than holistic or whole system relationships. On the other hand, many methods are subjective and rely on individual

Box 1.1 Methods of identifying risk

◆ Brainstorming
◆ Workshops
◆ Stakeholder consultations
◆ Benchmarking
◆ Checklists
◆ Scenario analysis
◆ Incident investigation
◆ Auditing and inspection
◆ Hazard and operability studies (HAZOP)
◆ Fish bone: breaking down a business process into its component parts to examine all the risks to that process
◆ Questionnaires/surveys
◆ Interviews

Box 1.2 Methods to assess the severity of risks

◆ Information gathering (e.g. market survey, research and development)
◆ Scenario planning
◆ Soft systems analysis
◆ Computer simulations, e.g. Monte Carlo
◆ Decision trees
◆ Root cause analysis
◆ Fault tree/event tree analysis
◆ Dependency modelling
◆ Failure mode and effect analysis (FMEA)
◆ Human reliability analysis
◆ Sensitivity analysis
◆ Cost-benefit and risk-benefit analysis
◆ Real option modelling
◆ Software packages
◆ Delphi method
◆ Risk map
◆ SWOT or PEST analysis
◆ Hazard and operability studies (HAZOP)
◆ Statistical inference
◆ Measures of central tendency and dispersion

perceptions of risk (e.g. soft systems analysis, brainstorming, cost-benefit and risk-benefit analysis, Delphi, etc.). Others combine both, with subjective judgements reflected in probabilities (e.g. Monte Carlo simulations, sensitivity analysis).

A common way of mapping and assessing the significance of risks is through the likelihood/impact matrix. The likelihood of occurrence may be high, medium or low. Similarly, impact or consequences in terms of downside risk (threats) or upside risk (missed opportunities) may be high, medium or low. For many organizations, a 3×3 matrix of high/medium/low will suit their needs, while for others a 5×5 (or even 7×7) matrix may be used. By considering the likelihood and consequences of each of the risks, it should be possible for organisations to map their risk exposure and then consider how to evaluate those risks.

Risk evaluation is concerned with making decisions about the significance of risks faced by the organisation, whether those risks should be accepted or whether there should be an appropriate treatment or response. This involves comparing the risks faced by an organisation against its desired risk profile (or risk appetite).

Risk appetite is the amount of risk an organisation is willing to accept in pursuit of value and may be expressed as an acceptable balance between growth, risk and return. Risk appetite may be made explicit in organisational strategies, policies and procedures or it may be implicit, needing to be derived from an analysis of past organisational decisions and actions.

Risk treatment (or risk response) is the process of selecting and implementing measures to modify the risk. This may include risk control/mitigation, risk avoidance, risk transfer, risk financing (e.g. insurance), etc. In establishing a portfolio view of risk responses, management will recognise the diversity of responses and the effect on the organisation's risk tolerance. The basic principle of portfolio theory is that it is less risky to have diverse sources of income through a portfolio of assets or investments. Spreading investments reduces risk, but may also reduce the probability of higher gains.

Risk reporting is concerned with regular reports to the board and to stakeholders setting out the organisation's policies in relation to risk and enabling the monitoring of the effectiveness of those policies.

The Committee of Sponsoring Organisations of the Treadway Commission (COSO, 2003) published *Enterprise Risk Management Framework*. This was updated as an *Integrated Framework* in 2004 (Committee of Sponsoring Organisations of the Treadway Commission (COSO), 2004). COSO defined enterprise risk management as:

> a process, effected by an entity's board of directors, management and other personnel, applied in strategy setting and across the enterprise, designed to identify potential events that may affect the entity, and manage risks to be within its risk appetite, to provide reasonable assurance regarding the achievement of entity objectives.

This approach to enterprise risk management was intended to align risk management with business strategy and embed a risk management culture into business operations. It encompassed the whole organisation and saw risks as opportunities to be grasped as much as hazards to be avoided. It is generally agreed among professional risk managers that the future management of risk will involve fostering a change in the risk culture of the organisation towards one where risks are considered as a normal part of the management process.

Risk culture may be regarded as the set of shared attitudes, values and practices that characterize how an entity considers risk in its day-to-day activities. This may be determined in part from the organisational vision and/or mission statement and strategy documents. However, it will be most clearly seen through organisational practices, notably rewards or sanctions for risk-taking or risk-avoiding behaviour. Both risk appetite and risk culture lead us to a consideration of the role of managers in relation to risk.

Managers and risk

Together with approaches that emphasise calculation, that is probability, sensitivity, hedging, insurance (itself based on probabilities), discount rates, etc., the assumption in much of the literature has been that risks can be assessed, measured and managed via feedback- and feed forward-type loops. However, many risks are not objectively identifiable and measurable but are subjective and qualitative. For example, the risks of litigation, economic downturns, loss of key employees, natural disasters, and loss of reputation are all subjective judgements. Risk is, therefore, to a considerable extent, 'socially constructed' and responses to risk reflect that social construction.

The view of risk as a systematic, rational device with tools and techniques to manage risk has been challenged (Beck, 1986/1992 in translation) with a wider view than the individual or the organisation. Beck's claim that we live in a 'risk society' was made from the stance that much risk was both part of the physical environment and also substantially created by the actions of companies, farmers and other actors. Further, the conceptions we have of risk are socially constructed. For something to be socially constructed is for meanings to be created and reinterpreted through social interaction, not just as a consequence of individual attitudes. Douglas and Wildavsky (1983) identified the perception of risk as a social process, with some risks being highlighted while others were downplayed.

Under an interpretive or social construction perspective, risk can be thought about by reference to:

◆ the existence of internal or external events
◆ information about those events (i.e. their visibility)
◆ managerial perception about events and information (i.e. how they are perceived)
◆ how organisations establish tacit/informal or explicit/formal ways of dealing with risk.

It has been argued (Bettis and Thomas, 1990) that researchers had very little knowledge about how managers in organisations perceived and took risks, or of the commonalities or differences between individual risk taking and risk taking by managers in the organisational context. Since then, in the last decade, there has been a myriad of publications on risk management by professional bodies and consulting firms and published research on various aspects of risk management, including technology (Shrivastava, 1993; Bussen and Myers, 1997; Kumar, 2002), outsourcing (Bhattacharya et al., 2003), reputation (Davies, 2002a), project management (Jiang and Klein, 1999; Miller and Lessard, 2001), and crisis (Davies, 2002b).

March and Shapira (1987) suggested that managers were insensitive to probabilities but were focused on performance in relation to critical performance targets. These authors identified three motivations for risk taking by managers. Managers saw risk taking as essential to success in decision-making; managers associated risk taking with the expectations of their jobs rather than with any personal preference for risk; and managers recognised the 'emotional pleasures and pains' of risk taking. As a result of their research, March and Shapira noted that both individual and institutionalised (i.e. taken for granted within the organisation) risk preferences were important in understanding organisational responses to risk management.

Adams (1995) developed the notion of the 'risk thermostat' to illustrate how everyone has a propensity to take risks, but the propensity to take risks varies from person to person. The propensity to take risks is influenced by the potential rewards of risk taking and perceptions of risk are also influenced by experience of 'accidents' that cause losses. Hence, according to Adams, individual risk taking represents a balance between perceptions of risk and the propensity to take risks with accident and losses as one consequence of taking risks. The risk thermostat has cultural filters through which risk/reward trade-offs and perceptions of danger/accidents are balanced.

Some of these perceptions may be based on national cultures, while others are organisational and/or individual. Uncertainty avoidance was one of the dimensions in the study on national cultural differences among IBM employees carried out by Hofstede (1980). The characteristic of uncertainty avoidance indicated the extent to which members of a society felt threatened by uncertainty and ambiguity. This was associated with seeing uncertainty as a threat, but compensated for by hard work, written rules and a belief in experts. In a comparative study of four cultures (American, German, Polish, and Chinese), Weber and Hsee (1998) found that the majority of respondents in all four cultures were perceived to be risk averse. These authors proposed a 'cushion hypothesis' because, in some countries (notably Chinese), collectivism cushions members against the consequences of negative outcomes. This in turn affects the subjective perceptions of the riskiness of options.

At the organisational level, Douglas and Wildavsky (1983) explained risk perception as a cultural process, commenting that each culture, each set of shared values and supporting social institutions, was biased toward highlighting certain risks and downplaying others. Adams (1995) also adopted a 'cultural theory' perspective and differentiated the formal sector of risk management, with its concern with risk reduction, from the informal sector of individuals seeking to balance risks with rewards. Adams, like others, also contrasted the distinction between objective, measurable risk and subjective, perceived risk.

Weber and Milliman (1997) described risk preference as a personal trait on a continuum from risk avoiding to risk taking, with risk factors being based on the magnitude of potential losses and their chances of occurring. They found that risk preference may be a stable personality trait, but the effect of situational variables on choice may be the result of changes in risk perception. These situational variables may exist at both national and organisational levels.

A survey of managers and accountants by Helliar et al. (2002) took a psychological approach to risk and found that loss aversion was dominant in decision-makers' minds. Probabilistic measures were not used as managers preferred to rely on instinct and experience which was then tested against corporate procedures to minimise risk. Helliar et al. (2001) found that, in some circumstances, managers were unable to distinguish between the risks that they were taking in their personal capacity and the risks they were taking on behalf of organisations. The managers in failing firms often focused on only one or two issues and were sometimes unable to separate their personal risks from business risks. They were willing to take gambles that might save their business from insolvency although, when threatened, their risk attitudes became more risk averse. Managers in turnaround activities were willing to ask for help sooner and recognized the need for action, demonstrating a more secure personal position.

Harris (1999, 2000) also drew on psychological theories in developing a project risk assessment framework to study risk assessment in capital investment decision-making, in which managers used a range of analytical tools to assess the likely risks and returns. Managers also drew upon their intuition and influenced others involved in the decision process. This suggested a link between human capabilities and procedures.

In their study of risk in budgeting, Collier and Berry (2002) argued that by excluding some risks and considering others, the process of constructing a budget was seen to be different to, and needed to be interpreted separately from, the content of the budget document in which there was little evidence of risk modelling or the use of probabilities.

Following Douglas and Wildavsky, Adams identified four distinctive world views that have important implications for risk. Adams' 'four rationalities' were: fatalists, hierarchists, individualists, and egalitarians.

◆ Fatalists have minimal control over their own lives and belong to no groups that are responsible for the decisions that rule their lives. They are resigned to their fate and see no point in trying to change it. Managing risks is irrelevant to fatalists.

◆ Hierarchists inhabit a world with strong group boundaries with social relationships being hierarchical. Hierarchists are always evident in large organisations with strong structures, procedures and systems. Hierarchists are most comfortable with a bureaucratic risk management style using various risk management techniques.

◆ Individualists are enterprising, self-made people, relatively free from control by others, but who strive to exert control over their environment. Entrepreneurs in small-medium enterprises fit into this category. Risk management to individualists is typically intuitive rather than systematic.

◆ Egalitarians have strong group loyalties but little respect for externally imposed rules and group decisions are arrived at democratically. Egalitarians are more commonly found in public sector and not-for-profit organisations whose values are oriented to social concerns. Egalitarians are most comfortable in situations of risk sharing through insurance, hedging or transfer to other organisations.

Figure 1.1 represents an adaptation from these four ideal types – which, in this research, was deemed an organisational risk stance – based on perspectives as to whether risk management is largely about avoiding negative consequences or achieving positive consequences.

The term 'egalitarian' has been replaced by the term 'Risk aware' to describe organisations that might be high on both aspects of risk management approach and which also attempt to build a culture of

	Risk management is about avoiding negative consequences	
	Low	High
Low	Risk sceptical	Hierarchists
Risk management is about achieving positive consequences		
High	Entrepreneurs	Risk aware

Figure 1.1 Ideal types applied to risk management stances. (Based on Adams, 1995 and Douglas and Wildavsky, 1983)

risk management into their operations. By contrast, the term 'fatalist' has been replaced by 'Risk sceptical' to reflect those organisations that do not believe that risk management is at all important. Managerial perceptions of risk lie at the heart of our study and the notions of the risk thermostat and the four rationalities of Adams (1995) will be revisited later in this book.

Risk and control

Internal control is the whole system of internal controls, financial and otherwise, established in order to provide reasonable assurance of effective and efficient operation, internal financial control, and compliance with laws and regulations (CIMA official terminology).

Like the report by International Federation of Accountants (1999), the guidance in the Turnbull Report (Institute of Chartered Accountants in England & Wales, 1999) emphasised that as profits are, in part, the reward for successful risk taking in business, the purpose of internal control is to help manage and control risk appropriately rather than to eliminate it. The *Combined Code on Corporate Governance* (Financial Reporting Council, 2003) encompassed the Turnbull Guidance, which provided that boards should maintain a sound system of internal control to safeguard shareholders' investment and the company's assets.

The Turnbull Guidance was based on the adoption by a company's board of a risk-based approach to establishing a sound system of internal control and reviewing its effectiveness (para. 9). Code C.2.1 of the Combined Code relates to internal control and provides that boards should conduct, at least annually, a review of the effectiveness of the group's system of internal controls and should report to shareholders that they have done so. This review should cover all material controls, including financial, operational and compliance controls and risk management systems.

In its *Enterprise Risk Management – Integrated Framework*, Committee of Sponsoring Organisations of the Treadway Commission (COSO) (COSO, 2004) developed a model of internal control containing eight components: internal environment; objective setting; event identification; risk assessment; risk response; control activities; information and communication; and monitoring.

1. The internal environment sets the basis for how risk is viewed and the organisational appetite for risk.
2. Organisational objectives must be consistent with risk appetite.
3. Events affecting achievement of objectives must be identified, distinguishing between risks and opportunities.
4. Risk assessment involves the analysis of risks into their likelihood and impact in order to determine how they should be managed.
5. Management then selects risk responses in terms of how risks may be mitigated, transferred or held.
6. Control activities in the form of policies and procedures ensure that risk responses are carried out effectively.
7. Information needs to be captured and communicated as the basis for risk management.
8. The enterprise risk management system should be regularly monitored and evaluated.

There has been an implicit assumption in much research that management control systems play an important part in risk management. However, Marshall et al. (1996: p.90) argued that an emphasis on internal control systems was insufficient because while information can be provided, decision-makers need knowledge to interpret that information, and an excess of controls can produce:

> an illusion of control; hiding the very real risks that lie in those areas where much that was not quantifiable or constant must be factored into a decision.

Berry et al. (2005) argued that the risk of control could be identified in a turbulent environment, where organisational participants may have less room to manoeuvre if they are prescriptive, leading to insufficient flexibility to cope with the unexpected. The existence of controls may themselves lead managers to believe that risks are well controlled and unforeseen circumstances may arise, or opportunities missed, because of an over-reliance on controls.

Spira and Page (2003) argued that the corporate governance framework was designed to manage risk through the accountability mechanisms of financial reporting, audit and internal control, in which internal auditors aspire to the reframing of their role in terms of risk management. Developments in corporate governance reporting offer opportunities for the appropriation of risk and its management by groups wishing to advance their own interests by asserting their own conceptions of risk and how it should be managed in an environment in which the failure to achieve corporate objectives provides a natural focus for risk management.

The changing role of management accountants

Management accounting is the application of the principles of accounting and financial management to create, protect, preserve and increase value so as to deliver that value to the stakeholders (CIMA *Official Terminology*).

Management accounting is concerned with information used in:

◆ Formulating business strategy
◆ Planning and controlling activities
◆ Decision-making
◆ Efficient resource usage
◆ Performance improvement and value enhancement
◆ Safeguarding tangible and intangible assets
◆ Corporate governance and internal control.

Consequently, either explicitly or implicitly, management accountants are involved in internal control mechanisms.

A study of changing management accounting practice on *The Future Direction of UK Management Accounting Practice* identified a change in the way management accounting was being used in organisations, from a traditional monitoring and control perspective to a more business and support-oriented perspective (Scapens et al., 2003). This research identified how many routine management accounting tasks either were being done by computer systems or by small, specialist groups. These authors argued that the challenge for the management accounting profession was to ensure that their members have the knowledge, skills and capabilities to take advantage of the opportunities that are undoubtedly there. The impact on management accountants identified by the Scapens et al. research study included:

- Database technologies which have facilitated the storage of vast quantities of information that is easily accessible and analysable. Transaction processing and routine management information was now computerised in most organisations.
- Decentring of accounting knowledge to non-financial managers who need to be aware of the financial consequences of their decisions. Cost management was increasingly seen as a management rather than an accounting task.
- Budgets were increasingly being used as flexible rather than static plans, being updated with rolling forecasts by managers for performance monitoring purposes.

These factors have led to a shift in the 'ownership' of accounting reports, from accountants to business managers. ₀

Scapens et al. argued that a key role for management accountants in the twenty-first century was integrating different sources of information and explaining the interconnections between non-financial performance measures and management accounting information. This would enable individual managers to see the linkages between their day-to-day operations, how these operations are presented in the monthly management accounts, and how they link to the broader strategic concerns of the business as reflected in the non-financial measures. Although Scapens et al. did not address the management accountant's role in risk management, each of the above roles implicitly involves accountants to a greater or lesser extent in identifying and managing risk. In an earlier study, Parker (2001) specifically noted the emerging role of accountants in risk management.

The Chartered Institute of Management Accountants (1999) report on *Corporate Governance: History, Practice and Future* viewed the role of management accountants in corporate governance as providing information to the chief executive and the board which allows their responsibilities to be effectively discharged.

CIMA's Fraud and Risk Management Working Group produced a guide to good practice in risk management (Chartered Institute of Management Accountants, 2002). The report argued that management accountants, whose professional training included the analysis of information and systems, performance and strategic management, can have a significant role to play in developing and implementing risk management and internal control systems within their organisations.

Summary

This chapter has given a brief overview of the practitioner literature on corporate governance, risk and risk management and an overview of the academic literature in relation to managers, risk, and control. It was complemented by some consideration of the changing requirements of management accountants.

Risk management is the process by which organisations methodically address the risks attaching to their activities with the goal of achieving sustained benefit within each activity in pursuit of organisational objectives and across the portfolio of all activities. The focus of good risk management is the identification and treatment of these risks consistent with the organisation's risk appetite. Valuable frameworks exist for risk management:

◆ The *Risk Management Standard* (Institute of Risk Management, 2002)
◆ *Enterprise Risk Management – Integrated Framework*, Committee of Sponsoring Organisations of the Treadway Commission (COSO, 2004)
◆ *Enterprise Governance: Getting the Balance Right* (CIMA, 2003).

In theoretical terms, a distinction has been made between event-uncertainty, commonly viewed as risk, and information-uncertainty (Galbraith, 1977). Two of Galbraith's four organisational design strategies, the creation of slack resources, and the creation of self-contained tasks reduce the need for information processing because of lower performance standards. The other two, investing in vertical information systems, and creating lateral relations increase the organisational capacity to process information.

Risk can be thought about by reference to the existence of internal or external events, information about those events (i.e. their visibility), managerial perception about events and information (i.e. how they are perceived), and how organisations establish tacit/informal or explicit/formal ways of dealing with risk. There is a distinction between objective, measurable risk and subjective, perceived risk.

Research shows that we know little about how managers consider risks (Bettis and Thomas, 1990) but managers do take risks, based on risk preferences at individual and organisational levels (March and Shapira, 1987). Some of these risk preferences vary with national cultures (Hofstede, 1980; Weber and Hsee, 1998). Some are individual traits (Weber and Milliman, 1997).

The 'risk thermostat' (Adams, 1995) recognizes that risk propensity varies based on the risk/reward trade-off and how these are balanced against perceptions of danger. Douglas and Wildavsky (1983) explained risk perception as a cultural process, commenting that each culture, each set of shared values and supporting social institutions is biased toward highlighting certain risks and downplaying others. We termed this the 'social construction' of risks.

We adapted the four 'ideal types' developed by Adams (1995): fatalists (or risk sceptical), hierarchists, individualists, and egalitarians (or risk aware), as 'risk stances' as a means of exploring and understanding individual and organisational risk management practices.

The *Combined Code on Corporate Governance* (Financial Reporting Council, 2003) is an important motivator for risk management and internal control practices. Internal control is the whole system of internal controls, financial and otherwise, established in order to provide reasonable assurance of effective and efficient operation, internal financial control, and compliance with laws and regulations. However, as profits are, in part, the reward for successful risk taking in business then the purpose of internal control is to help manage and control risk appropriately rather than to eliminate it. Nevertheless, there is the possibility of the illusion of control. The changing role of management accountants is also an important factor in establishing the context for their role in risk management and wider views of management control.

Exploratory case studies

Purpose

The purpose of the exploratory case studies was to understand the relationship between risk and budgeting. This involved consideration of how risk was enacted in budgeting and how managerial perceptions of risk influenced the process and content of budgets. The study was designed to explore the observation made by Berry et al. (1995) that:

> what one sees in a financial plan, especially one which is projected on a spreadsheet as single-point estimates over ten years, might be one where the problem of uncertainty has been set aside.

Discussions of risk in management accounting texts are most commonly linked to rational concepts and the use of probability, primarily in the context of capital budgeting decisions, to reflect unpredictability. *Risk modelled* budgeting was conjectured as a descriptive model of the environment–organisation interface through input–output modelling which assumes knowledge of the means–ends transformation process.

On the other hand, observation of practice has revealed that organisations may conceive of the budgetary system as a rational system and seek to close it off from external influence. Budgets are often single-point estimates rather than a range of possible outcomes determined through sensitivity analysis. In essence, this is a budgetary system designed within an implicit protective boundary. Here, risk is explicitly excluded from the budgetary system and is managed in some other domain. Hence, the *risk excluded* form of budget was proposed.

Where organisations give attention to environmental influences, while simultaneously creating a protective boundary, albeit in different elements of the budgetary system, a *risk considered* form of budgeting was conjectured.

Research design

The exploratory case study was chosen as the most suitable method because it enabled a study of the budgeting process and the perceptions of various organisational participants as distinct from the content of budgetary documents.

The selection of cases included both business and not-for-profit sectors. Within the business sector, the researchers wanted to consider separately large and smaller organisations. Within the not-for-profit sector, the researchers wanted to study a public sector organisation and a voluntary organisation. By selecting four very different organisations, the researchers' intent was to identify any similarities and differences in approaches to risk in the process of budgeting.

The study was a pilot study funded by the Chartered Institute of Management Accountants (CIMA) and conducted in each of the four organisations during 2000. These organisations are referred to as S, T, P and Q respectively. S was a plant of a multinational Fortune 500 automotive parts supplier, an assembler and sequencer of parts for a single customer, which exhibited the characteristics of a multinational. T was a manufacturing firm, a subsidiary of an unlisted management buyout. P was a non-metropolitan police force. Q was a voluntary sector organisation that provided both direct services to clients through funded projects and contributed to national policy debates. The major form of data collection was from interviews during site visits with some observation.

These cases were not selected to be in any way representative of larger groups, but as diverse organisations that might illustrate different approaches to risk and budgeting. They were, however, all parts of larger national organisations. This resulted in the (deliberate) exclusion of financial market issues from the study.

The detailed research results were published by Elsevier in *Management Accounting Research* (Collier and Berry, 2002).

Research findings

Risk

At the time of the research visits it was observed that each of the case study organisations was facing a mini-crisis involving risk. S was in negotiations with its single customer. Managers in T were expressing significant concerns over the viability of the business in the face of a steady decline in sales and poor delivery performance. P had presented options to its police authority in relation to the precept – the police component of the council tax – that would determine the number of police officers. Q faced press reports and public anger about paedophile activity that influenced fund raising and public support. Each example enhanced the interviewees' general perceptions of risk with situation-specific illustrations of risk as it pertained to the process and content of the budget.

The consequences of risk varied for each organisation. For S, financial risk was high for the plant studied due to its dependence on a single customer, although it shared operational risk with its logistics and computer systems suppliers. However for S's parent, the plant was only one among many. For T, the principal risk was the removal of financial support by institutional investors or, operationally, the degradation of customer satisfaction with delivery such that the level of business would continue to decline. For P the risk, given a cash-limited budget, was the inability to satisfy public demand given the 'squeeze' on resources and the local political impact of the trade-off between police numbers and an increased council tax levy. For Q, the primary risks were to its reputation as a result of press coverage and the consequential risk to the continuity of funding, as well as the personal risk to employees and volunteers coping with high levels of stress and anxiety.

Budgets

In each case, the researchers asked interviewees about the process of budgeting that was used in their organisations. It became evident in each organisation that, despite managerial perceptions of risk, these perceptions were not evident in the budget process or the content of the budget document. In S and T, top-down budgets were established by the parent boards with no explicit regard to risk. In P, once the budget was set by the police authority, there was little financial risk due to the predictability of cash flows. In Q, budgeting took place within known grants and resource allocations from the national body.

In each case, budgeting was top-down, driven either by targets or cash limits. Despite the managerial perceptions of risk that covered wide-ranging issues, the budgeting process was largely protected from the influence of those perceptions. It was as though the budget, with well understood imperfections, was a point of stability in turbulent worlds. In all four cases the process was of risk exclusion from budgets, but not from the processes of budgeting.

Risk construction and domains of risk

Risk was constructed by managers of S in a narrow sense, mainly from a technological, systems-based perspective. This was a result of the finite boundaries that had been put around the business unit, first, as a single customer plant and secondly, as a subsidiary of a Fortune 500 company. In S, operational and financial risk was inter-related. The single customer risk was offset in contractual terms that minimised volume variations and passed on price increases during the contract period. The most substantial risk, of contract failure, was insignificant given S was a business unit of a multinational company. Financial risk in terms of the expected return, while not meeting parent targets, was considered satisfactory because there was little investment in plant and lease obligations could be passed to the customer given six months' notice of termination.

T's boundaries were defined by the exit strategy of its investor and also in relation to the organisation's history, technology and product range being out of step with market changes. This may be evidence of a prior process of mis-construction of risk. There was evidence from the interviews that understanding of risk was being recon-structed before, during and presumably after the time of the study. The main risks to T were the loss of investor support and retaining sales in a very competitive market. These risks were exacerbated by the poor flexibility evident in its equipment capability and the work-ing practices of its employees, together with difficulties that had led to poor delivery performance that could easily result in lost business.

The construction of risk was also a continuing aspect of P's world that combined uncertain demand, limited resources and unclear and ambiguous relationships between inputs and outcomes. P was continually aware of the social and political risks that were associ-ated with national expectations of productivity improvements and financial constraints. In P, the research identified the notional sep-aration of operational and financial risk, given the absence of con-nection between demand and resources. These were becoming more closely connected as the operational implications of financial constraint were being recognised. What was particularly evident in

P was the political risk in managing relations between the police force, the Home Office, the police authority and local authorities over decisions about the level of precept (tax).

Q understood how funding agencies and the public saw the issues with which they were trying to deal. For Q, risk was constructed in relation to clients and their families and in relation to the effect on staff. There was an enhanced awareness of organisational and personal functioning in relation to personal risk that fed into managerial processes and roles. In Q, the operational risk was evident in the need to maintain the organisation's reputation while simultaneously being innovative. Financial risk was represented by fund raising constraints imposed by the outcome rationality of funding agencies and perceptions of the public. Particularly evident was the need to balance the delivery of project outcomes with the personal risk to its staff and how this was addressed by training and by managers' monitoring how well staff handled difficult situations.

In each of the four organisations the context of unique circumstances, history and technology had led to different processes of construction of ideas about risk. In the private sector firms S and T, this came from a form of economic and technical rationality, themselves strongly influenced by economic ideology. In P and Q it came from social, political and ideological change.

The cases differently illustrated the manner in which organisations and their actors created domains in which risk could be understood and managed. Four domains of risk – financial, operational, political and personal – were found to exist and could be observed to each of the four cases, albeit in different degrees. Risk was perceived in each of these domains, but these domains were isolated from the budgeting process that was dominated by target setting or the imposition of cash limits. It was perhaps inevitable that these differing social constructions, reflected in different domains, led to differences between the process and content of budgeting.

Process and content of budgets

In S, the budgeting process reflected a compromise between the parent company targets and the single-customer volume and price negotiations. In T, the budgeting process was top-down, with sales projections driving standard production costs and profitability targets that had to meet short-term investor targets. In P, no representation of risk appeared in the budget, other than tacitly in the reserves carried forward at year-end. The calculations presented to the police authority did, however, reflect a consideration of the impact of various budgetary outcomes on the number of police officers, and hence – albeit implicitly – on operational effectiveness. In Q, financial risk was considered in the planning process both nationally and at the regional level, although the budgets were constructed on the basis of best estimates of funding and expenditure.

An analysis of these cases suggests that the process of budgeting and the resulting content of the budget may take any of the three forms identified earlier: risk excluded, risk considered or risk modelled. Using this schema, the process of budgeting in all four cases was characterised as risk considered, in which a top-down budgeting process reflected negotiated targets. The content of budget documents were risk excluded, being based on a set of single-point estimates, in which all of the significant risks were excluded from the budget itself. The one exception was P, in which there was evidence of risk considered processes in the papers prepared for the police authority for their decision about the precept. Risk consideration was also implicit in the reserves maintained by P for unpredictable operational and pension contingencies.

There was no evidence at the business unit level of any formal risk modelling and an absence of discussion about any input–output relationships. No manager, in any of the four cases, suggested any calculation or use of probabilities (as March and Shapira (1987) suggested). Some elements of risk modelling were possible – at least implicitly – within S, but only because the nature of its single-customer business with (± 3 per cent) volume certainty and the ability to pass most cost increases to the customer, provided the ability to predict most of the financial outcomes.

This suggests that budgeting, as a rational system, was separate from the managerial perspective (implied by the views of budget 'participants') that reflected the location of risk in the interface between organisation and environment. There are significant consequences for the management of risk in this separation as budgeting did not appear, in any of the four cases, to be a tool used in risk management, nor was risk evident in the risk excluded budgetary documents.

Summary of main case study findings

The findings from the four case studies reveal differences based on the contexts of unique circumstances, histories and technologies of the organisations. The four cases illustrate how the different social constructions of participants in the budgeting process influenced the domains – or alternative lenses – through which the process of budgeting took place and how the content of the budget was determined. However, the research identified some similarities in the four cases summarised as follows:

1. Four domains of risk were observed, reflecting the different social constructions of participants – financial, operational, political and personal. These domains were important in understanding how risk was perceived in the budgeting process. Risk was perceived in each of these domains, but these perceptions were isolated from the rational budgeting process that was dominated by top-down targets or cash limits.

2. As previously stated, the process and content of budgeting was categorised as risk modelled, risk considered or risk excluded. There was little direct evidence of risk modelling in the four cases and a minor reflection of risk consideration in one case. The *process* of budgeting in all four cases was characterised as risk considered, in which a top-down budgeting process reflected negotiated targets. The *content* of budget documents were risk excluded, being based on a set of single-point estimates, in which all of the significant risks were excluded from the budget itself. The separation of budgeting and risk management had significant consequences for the management of risk as the process of budgeting needs to be considered separately from the content of budget documents. This has implications for where risk is held within organisations.

3. Risk transfer took place between and within organisations. Risk transfer may be a response to avoid the problems implied by the separation of a budget that is risk excluded from a budgeting process that is risk considered. This response may be a reaction to the lack of 'participation' by budget holders and the risk perceptions held by managers.

4. Managers 'held' risk and provided containment for the anxiety of others. Risk containment is a particular type of risk transfer, from the organisation to its managers, which takes place in relation to

residual risks, not contained within the budget. Risk containment implies a significant personal burden on managers.

This research suggests that there is a relationship between the social constructions of budget participants at different levels of analysis that impacts upon the budgeting process. In particular, the process of budgeting, by excluding some risks and considering others, is seen to be different to, and needs to be interpreted separately from, the content of the budget. This observation is particularly relevant in observing how risk can shift between and within organisations and how managers may themselves hold risk on behalf of the organisation.

These issues are of particular importance given the requirements of the Turnbull Guidance (Institute of Chartered Accountants in England & Wales, 1999) subsequently incorporated into the *Combined Code on Corporate Governance* (Financial Reporting Council, 2003) for boards of directors to identify, evaluate and manage significant risks in their organisations. If, as the four cases suggest, the most significant risks may be excluded from financial reports, the requirements of governance and internal control suggest that the budget as a process needs to be better understood.

Following these observations, it was necessary to extend the study in two directions. The first of these was to undertake a single 'holistic' case study of one complex organisation in order to trace the processes of risk management and its relationship to accounting and to accountants. The other was to extend the general study across many organisations to test for a wider applicability and to include some further considerations of risk and its management. The latter course was followed and the next chapter reports on the design and findings from a survey project.

Survey research

Introduction

Following the case studies, it was decided to undertake a survey of organisations in the UK to examine risk management practices and the role of management accountants in risk management.

Solomon et al. (2000) built on the Turnbull Report to develop a framework for internal control, risk management and risk disclosure. These research findings indicated that institutional investors do not favour a regulated environment for corporate risk disclosure or a general statement of business risk, although respondents agreed that increased risk disclosure would assist in portfolio investment decisions.

This chapter describes the survey design, the survey instrument, the method of analysis and the results of that analysis.

Survey design

Risk management practices

Much of the financial and governance literature rests in the tradition of normative theorising or injunction. There was little research that set out to explain the degree to which the organisational practice of risk management was influenced by considerations of economic rationality and corporate governance. The research reported here aimed to understand the drivers and practice of risk management and the consequences for performance for the organisations. A subsidiary theme was the role of accountants in risk management. The research builds on prior research in this area, such as that by Helliar et al. (2002).

From rational considerations it was conjectured that risk management practices would be a function of the degree of environmental uncertainty which organisations perceive to be affecting them. It was expected that the higher the degree of environmental uncertainty then the more complex and advanced would be risk management practices.

Hence, we sought to observe:

1. The use of basic methods of risk management (Q2.18; 5 elements; 5 pt scale)

2. The use of advanced methods of risk management (Q2.18; 3 elements; 5 pt scale)
3. The perceived degree of environmental uncertainty faced by the organisation (Q2.6; 4 elements; 5 pt scale).

(References here are to particular questions in the survey instrument, see Appendix 1).

It was conjectured that risk management practices would be a function of the *risk stance* of the organisation. The risk stance of the organisation was inferred from the degree to which organisational risk management was designed to take advantage of risk as opportunity (an economic rationale, and corporate governance rationale) and the degree to which organisational risk management was designed to provide protection from risk (corporate governance rationale). The risk management stances were derived from Douglas and Wildavsky and Adams and are shown in Figure 1.1 (see p. 18). It was decided to change the Douglas and Wildavsky term 'egalitarian' and substitute the term 'risk aware' to describe organisations that might be high on both aspects of the risk management approach and to use the term 'risk sceptical' (rather than fatalist) to describe organisations that would score low on both aspects.

Hence, we also sought to observe:

4. The degree to which the organisation's risk management was designed to protect the organisation (Q2.12; 5 pt scale)
5. The degree to which the organisation's risk management was designed to take advantage of opportunities (Q2.12; 5 pt scale).

To check respondent bias we sought individual respondents' views of these two questions (Q1.4; 5 pt scales).

It was observed from the case studies that risk was absent from the formal financial statements but considered in the processes of financial management. Hence, to approach this finding it was decided to observe whether risk was considered in the processes of planning. The case studies had indicated that risk management may have some supporting policies. Hence, we sought to observe:

6. The degree to which risks were 'factored into' organisational planning (Q2.19; 6 elements; 5 pt scales)

7. The degree to which there were supporting policies and culture (Q2.9; 9 elements; 5 pt scale).

There have been very few studies (if any) which have been able to measure the consequences for organisational performance arising from risk management practices. Hence, we sought to observe:

8. The degree to which risk management practices have led to improved performance (Q2.21; 6 elements; 5 pt scale).

Corporate governance is substantially directed to improving the relationship with stakeholders and perhaps involving stakeholders in corporate management. Hence, we sought to observe:

9. The degree to which stakeholders were involved in risk management in the organisation (Q2.15; 4 elements; 5 pt scales) and
10. The degree to which risk management practices have led to improved relationships with stakeholders (Q2.21; 3 elements; 5 pt scales).

The conjectured relationships are shown in Figure 3.1.

It has been observed that individual and organisations may be held to have a propensity for taking risks – a risk 'appetite'. Hence, we sought to observe:

11. The individual and organisational propensity to take risks (Q1.2, 1.3, 2.10 and 2.11; 2 elements in each; 5 pt scales).

Figure 3.1 Conjectured relationships in our study

In order to ascertain organisations' perceptions of the 'drivers' of risk management, we sought to observe:

12. Organisation's perceptions of the significance of a range of risk drivers: legislation, regulatory bodies, expectations of share-holders and analysts, competitive business environment, customers/clients, critical events, and the board (Q2.8; 5 pt scales).

Finally, in order to examine whether organisational size or type (private sector, public sector, manufacturing or service provision) affected risk management practices, we sought to observe:

13. Age, size and type of organisation (Q2.1, 2.2, 2.3, 2.4, and 2.5; single item responses).

The role of accountants in risk management

The role of accountants in risk management was a subsidiary theme. This was not to discount the importance of financial accountants in the disclosure of risk (following Solomon et al., 2000), but reflected the role of management accountants in risk-based internal control (after Spira and Page, 2003). Hence, we sought to observe:

1. The job title of the person primarily accountable for four elements of risk management: identifying, analysing and assessing, deciding on action, reporting and monitoring risks (Q2.14; 8 elements; single response)
2. The degree of involvement of management accountants in risk management (Q2.17; 2 elements; 4 pt scale)
3. The integration of management accounting and risk management functions (Q2.16; 5 pt scale).

In addition to these items, we sought observations on:

4. Trends in risk management practice, past, present and future (Q2.13; 4 elements; 3 pt scale)
5. The use of risk management approaches of transferring, reducing and mitigating (Q 2.20, 2 elements; 5 pt scales)
6. The perceived relationship of costs and benefits of risk management (Q. 2.22; 5 pt scales).

The survey design is shown diagrammatically in Figure 3.2. Our framework suggested that risk management practices in organisations would likely be adopted and maintained as a consequence of various drivers: external regulation, environmental factors, demographic factors and the organisational risk propensity (or appetite). The role of management accountants in risk management was a subsidiary theme. Finally, the perceived effectiveness of risk management practices was sought.

The survey instrument

As part of the design process, six interviews were conducted with managers responsible for risk management. In addition, there was an interview with the chief executive of a professional association of risk managers. The research instruments were tested for comprehension on ten respondents, which included all those we had interviewed as part of the survey design process as well as other respondents we approached who had no involvement in the survey design. Following advice from interviewees, the survey

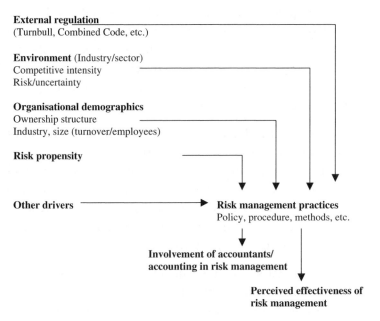

Figure 3.2 Framework for risk management practices in organisations

was compressed into a four page printed document (see Appendix 1) in order to make it easier to answer and hence improve the response rate.

In line with research intent, the survey was directed to three groups: large publicly quoted companies (FTSE), small and medium sized organisations (SMEs) and accountants (CIMA members). Survey responses in most cases required respondents to tick a box on a 5-point Likert scale. There were two separate survey instruments, although there were only minor differences between the two, to reflect the knowledge that all CIMA members were accountants, which modified two of the questions.

The research was undertaken using a postal survey instrument mailed to 3000 named people, (2000 CIMA members; 500 FTSE Directors and 500 SME Directors). CIMA produced a mailing list of 5000 members based in the UK who had been members for more than 3 years and had the word 'accountant' in their job title. We randomly selected two from every five. For the FTSE sample we obtained the details of UK companies listed on the London Stock Exchange from www.londonstockexchange.com. Companies listed on the Alternative Investment Market, Investment Companies and Investment Entities were excluded, leaving a population of 1179. These companies were arranged alphabetically and 500 companies were randomly selected. The financial director's name was used in the first instance, but if this was unavailable, the chief executive's name was used. The covering letter accompanying the questionnaire asked the named person or a nominee from their senior management teams to complete the questionnaire.

Using FAME, UK SMEs were identified with a minimum turnover of between £2 million and £11.2 million and a minimum number of 50 employees. This effectively eliminated the very small business sector and is in line with the Companies Act definition of an SME. Five hundred companies were selected randomly from a total population of 19 811 and the survey was addressed to the named chief executive or managing director.

From the postal survey instrument targeted at the three groups – stock exchange listed companies (FTSE), small & medium enterprises (SMEs) and CIMA members – there were 333 usable responses, a rate of 11 per cent which was deemed adequate to enable analysis, particularly as there were sufficient responses over each of the three survey groups to provide statistical tests. The responses are shown in Table 3.1.

An additional theme of the study was to explore whether the risk stance of the company was related to its market performance (valuation). However, in the survey, respondents were permitted to provide a response without identifying their organisation by name, hence, this additional part of the research was limited by the available data. It was conjectured that the risk stance would be associated with market valuation. Because risk awareness was considered to be a more sophisticated risk stance it was conjectured that the risk aware companies would be favourably viewed by the market.

Survey analysis

In this report, the different survey group responses are largely omitted except where they are relevant to the conclusions drawn.

The raw survey data was entered into SPSS and examined to check the distributions of the scales. A preliminary statistical analysis suggested that the scale elements for the variable under examination were highly correlated. Factor analysis was used on the raw data which produced 'group' responses for the variables. These items were subjected to principal components analysis using SPSS. Cronbach's alpha coefficient was used to measure the internal consistency of the eleven 'groups' (Table 3.2). Based upon the new

Table 3.1 Summary of survey responses

	Sample			
	CIMA	*FTSE*	*SME*	*Total*
Questionnaires issued	2000	500	500	3000
Total responses	259	63	47	369
Response rate (%)	13	12.6	9.4	12.3
Non-usable responses	17	13	6	36
Usable responses	242	50	41	333
Usable response rate (%)	12.1	10.0	8.2	11.1

group variables, comparisons of the responses of CIMA, FTSE and SME groups were made. Following the statistical analysis, the findings were explored with a small number of risk management professionals, management accountants and SME managers who

Table 3.2   Factor analysis

Group construct description	Factor analysis			
	No.of items	Cronbach's alpha	Mean	Std dev.
Total sample				
1 Degree of uncertainty & risk faced	3	0.7985	3.46	0.71
2 Change in uncertainty & risk faced	3	0.8039	3.84	0.60
3 Supporting processes and culture	8	0.8833	3.44	0.67
4 Stakeholder involvement	4	0.6806	2.87	0.78
5 Usage rate of basic methods	4	0.6696	2.76	0.87
6 Usage rate of technical methods	2	0.7590	1.91	0.99
7 Effectiveness of basic methods	4	0.6913	2.75	0.87
8 Effectiveness of technical methods	2	0.7735	2.01	1.02
9 Risks factored into organisational planning	6	0.8784	3.37	0.83
10 Improved performance	9	0.8942	2.93	0.72
11 Improved external relationships	3	0.8131	2.49	0.89
CIMA				
1 Degree of uncertainty & risk faced	3	0.7900	3.44	0.73
2 Change in uncertainty & risk faced	3	0.7983	3.89	0.59
3 Supporting processes and culture	8	0.8867	3.37	0.69
4 Stakeholder involvement	4	0.6728	2.87	0.76
5 Usage rate of basic methods	4	0.6961	2.72	0.89
6 Usage rate of technical methods	2	0.7423	2.02	1.03
7 Effectiveness of basic methods	4	0.7324	2.68	0.89
8 Effectiveness of technical methods	2	0.7688	2.13	1.06
9 Risks factored into organisational planning	6	0.8795	3.26	0.83
10 Improved performance	9	0.8937	2.87	0.72
11 Improved external relationships	3	0.8275	2.50	0.90
FTSE				
1 Degree of uncertainty & risk faced	3	0.8098	3.59	0.68
2 Change in uncertainty & risk faced	3	0.8602	3.73	0.63
3 Supporting processes and culture	8	0.8111	3.66	0.50
4 Stakeholder involvement	4	0.7415	2.83	0.84
5 Usage rate of basic methods	4	0.5107	3.04	0.78
6 Usage rate of technical methods	2	0.7989	1.70	0.93
7 Effectiveness of basic methods	4	0.4644	3.10	0.72
8 Effectiveness of technical methods	2	0.7739	1.85	0.99

Table 3.2 *(Continued)*

Group construct description	Factor analysis			
	No.of items	*Cronbach's alpha*	*Mean*	*Std dev.*
9 Risks factored into organisational planning	6	0.8595	3.58	0.75
10 Improved performance	9	0.8876	2.95	0.71
11 Improved external relationships	3	0.8137	2.36	0.92
SME				
1 Degree of uncertainty & risk faced	3	0.8456	3.46	0.69
2 Change in uncertainty & risk faced	3	0.7352	3.67	0.60
3 Supporting processes and culture	8	0.8901	3.58	0.62
4 Stakeholder involvement	4	0.6497	2.90	0.81
5 Usage rate of basic methods	4	0.6494	2.70	0.85
6 Usage rate of technical methods	2	0.7826	1.54	0.61
7 Effectiveness of basic methods	4	0.5892	2.72	0.83
8 Effectiveness of technical methods	2	0.7873	1.60	0.72
9 Risks factored into organisational planning	6	0.8723	3.70	0.76
10 Improved performance	9	0.8924	3.23	0.66
11 Improved external relationships	3	0.7224	2.61	0.78

Std dev. : standard deviation

helped to inform the interpretation of, and explanations for the statistical results.

The relationships between the grouped variables were investigated for the total responses and each of the survey groups. Chi-square tests were used to analyse relations between categorical variables such as risk propensity and survey family. We also used one-way ANOVA (analysis of variance) to determine if there were any significant differences in mean scores across the three survey groups. Spearman's rank order correlation (rho) was used to calculate the strength of relationship between the groups, which are shown in Table 3.3. The correlations present what appears to be a coherent view of risk taken by respondents. The correlations also suggest that respondents had a commonality of view of notions of uncertainty and risk.

Appendix 2 contains more detailed statistical information in relation to those tables in the text which contain only mean and standard deviation data.

Table 3.3 Correlations of grouped responses

		1	2	3	4	5	6	7	8	9	10
Total sample											
Degree of uncertainty & risk faced	1										
Change in uncertainty & risk faced	2	0.295**									
Supporting processes & culture	3	0.111*	-0.087								
Stakeholder involvement	4	0.083	-0.032	0.078							
Usage rate of basic methods	5	0.023	0.055	0.497**	0.095						
Usage rate of technical methods	6	0.120*	0.050	0.373**	0.246**	0.508**					
Effectiveness of basic methods	7	-0.057	0.017	0.463**	0.102	0.847**	0.447**				
Effectiveness of technical methods	8	0.062	0.015	0.302**	0.216**	0.425**	0.836**	0.525**			
Risks factored into organisational planning	9	0.083	-0.065	0.398**	0.212**	0.320**	0.301**	0.313**	0.268**		
RM has improved performance	10	0.080	0.040	0.491**	0.205**	0.357**	0.423**	0.366**	0.333**	0.455**	
RM has improved external relationships	11	0.055	-0.047	0.289**	0.466**	0.290**	0.411**	0.339**	0.364**	0.264**	0.606**
CIMA											
Degree of uncertainty & risk faced	1										
Change in uncertainty & risk faced	2	0.280**									
Supporting processes & culture	3	0.092	-0.054								
Stakeholder involvement	4	0.098	-0.062	0.102							
Usage rate of basic methods	5	0.016	0.095	0.505**	0.054						
Usage rate of technical methods	6	0.141*	0.038	0.435**	0.251**	0.550**					
Effectiveness of basic methods	7	-0.051	0.059	0.466**	0.101	0.848**	0.507**				
Effectiveness of technical methods	8	0.023	-0.035	0.388**	0.261**	0.498**	0.845**	0.593**			

	#	1	2	3	4	5	6	7	8	9	10
Risks factored into organisational planning	9	0.094	-0.041	0.431**	0.272**	0.342**	0.450**	0.327**	0.422**		
RM has improved performance	10	0.070	0.046	0.524**	0.238**	0.359***	0.511***	0.385***	0.434***	C.484**	
RM has improved external relationships	11	0.080	-0.035	0.306**	0.442**	0.273**	0.414**	0.337**	0.406**	C.325**	0.643**
FTSE											
Degree of uncertainty & risk faced	1										
Change in uncertainty & risk faced	2	0.261									
Supporting processes & culture	3	0.160	-0.022								
Stakeholder involvement	4	0.107	0.052	0.171							
Usage rate of basic methods	5	-0.007	0.102	0.436**	0.184						
Usage rate of technical methods	6	0.255	0.193	0.531**	0.257	0.420**					
Effectiveness of basic methods	7	-0.078	0.064	0.359*	-0.005	0.789**	0.344*				
Effectiveness of technical methods	8	0.454**	0.218	0.364*	0.101	0.267	0.840**	0.390**			
Risks factored into organisational planning	9	-0.122	-0.150	0.284	0.024	0.044	0.050	0.095	0.019		
RM has improved performance	10	0.079	0.039	0.495**	0.262	0.330*	0.340*	0.214	0.190	C.337*	
RM has improved external relationships	11	-0.010	-0.061	0.504**	0.605**	0.305*	0.387**	0.326*	0.192	0.174	0.621**
SME											
Degree of uncertainty & risk faced	1										
Change in uncertainty & risk faced	2	0.529**									
Supporting processes & culture	3	0.135	-0.168								
Stakeholder involvement	4	-0.004	0.116	-0.146							
Usage rate of basic methods	5	0.043	-0.131	0.415**	0.188						
Usage rate of technical methods	6	-0.130	-0.284	0.178	0.339*	0.585**					

(Continued)

Table 3.3 (*Continued*)

		1	2	3	4	5	6	7	8	9	10
Effectiveness of basic methods	7	-0.132	-0.184	0.432**	0.231	0.878**	0.489**				
Effectiveness of technical methods	8	-0.175	-0.223	0.089	0.223	0.383*	0.745**	0.547**			
Risks factored into organisational planning	9	0.155	0.082	0.182	0.147	0.459**	0.146	0.384*	0.007		
RM has improved performance	10	0.047	0.109	0.258	-0.132	0.509**	0.321*	0.520**	0.313	0.318	
RM has improved external relationships	11	-0.046	-0.169	0.105	0.396*	0.516**	0.494**	0.543**	0.484**	0.176	0.399*

** Correlation is significant at the 0.01 level (2-tailed). * Correlation is significant at the 0.05 level (2-tailed)

Survey results

Demographics

There were no significant correlations between either the ownership structure of the organisation or the nature of business and any of the grouped data. We did find some significant positive correlations (at the 0.01 level) with the size of the organisation and the use of basic and sophisticated methods of risk assessment and management. There was therefore little evidence of any contingent explanations for risk management based on either size or business sector. This finding differed from the implication of that of Liebenberg and Hoyt (2003) who found no effect of size.

Environmental uncertainty

There was no significant correlation between environmental uncertainty and risk (or the change in uncertainty and risk) and other group variables. This negated one of the assumptions in the conceptual framework, that environmental uncertainty and risk would influence risk management practices. It is possible the respondents regarded the question as too abstract and would assume that the various aspects of the environment were subsumed in the manner in which risks were factored into planning.

Respondents rated competitive intensity and degree of uncertainty in their industry/sector, as well as the degree of risk faced by the organisation and the sector. This is shown in Table 3.4 (Appendix 2 contains expanded statistics for this table).

Overall, CIMA respondents were more risk concerned than the other respondent groups in relation to their organisations, despite having a lower perception of competitive intensity and uncertainty in their industry/sector.

Drivers of risk management

Table 3.5 shows that the strongest drivers of risk management were the board/top management, legislation and the competitive business environment. Appendix 2 contains expanded statistics for this table.

Table 3.4   Competitive intensity, uncertainty and risk

	*Mean	Std dev.
Total sample		
Degree of competitive intensity in the industry/sector	3.56	1.18
Degree of uncertainty in the industry/sector environment	3.43	0.94
Degree of risk faced by the organisation	3.46	0.81
Degree of risk faced within industry/sector	3.50	0.79
CIMA		
Degree of competitive intensity in the industry/sector	3.42	1.26
Degree of uncertainty in the industry/sector environment	3.37	0.96
Degree of risk faced by the organisation	3.45	0.83
Degree of risk faced within industry/sector	3.48	0.79
FTSE		
Degree of competitive intensity in the industry/sector	3.88	0.90
Degree of uncertainty in the industry/sector environment	3.59	0.81
Degree of risk faced by the organisation	3.54	0.76
Degree of risk faced within industry/sector	3.61	0.81
SME		
Degree of competitive intensity in the industry/sector	4.05	0.77
Degree of uncertainty in the industry/sector environment	3.56	0.90
Degree of risk faced by the organisation	3.37	0.70
Degree of risk faced within industry/sector	3.46	0.78

* 1 = very low; 5 = very high. Std dev.: standard deviation

There was general agreement in the responses that legislation, regulatory bodies, the board/top management and the competitive business environment were important drivers of risk management. This is in contrast to the finding above that competitive intensity was not an important driver. However, the high 'agree' response to all the drivers raises questions about the value of these responses. During follow-up interviews the importance of compliance with legislation as the dominant driver for many organisations was emphasised.

The extent to which shareholders and analysts, suppliers, customers, and banks and financiers were involved in risk management in the respondents' organisations is shown in Table 3.6 (Appendix 2 contains expanded statistics for this table).

These results suggested that risk management was driven by an institutional response to calls for improved corporate governance, which may reflect both protection and economic opportunity. The

Table 3.5 Drivers of risk management

	*Mean	Std dev.
Total sample		
Legislation (including Combined Code and Turnbull Report)	3.79	0.82
Regulatory bodies	3.79	0.83
Expectations of shareholders/analysts	3.35	0.98
The competitive business environment	3.72	0.79
Customers/clients who demand it	3.51	0.90
A critical event or a near miss	3.54	0.97
Board/top management	3.84	0.70
CIMA		
Legislation (including Combined Code and Turnbull Report)	3.80	0.81
Regulatory bodies	3.81	0.82
Expectations of shareholders/analysts	3.29	1.00
The competitive business environment	3.70	0.80
Customers/clients who demand it	3.63	0.85
A critical event or a near miss	3.60	0.98
Board/top management	3.82	0.70
FTSE		
Legislation (including Combined Code and Turnbull Report)	3.72	0.99
Regulatory bodies	3.64	0.94
Expectations of shareholders/analysts	3.66	0.89
The competitive business environment	3.66	0.87
Customers/clients who demand it	3.00	0.96
A critical event or a near miss	3.20	0.95
Board/top management	3.88	0.75
SME		
Legislation (including Combined Code and Turnbull Report)	3.80	0.68
Regulatory bodies	3.85	0.76
Expectations of shareholders/analysts	3.29	0.84
The competitive business environment	3.88	0.56
Customers/clients who demand it	3.41	0.92
A critical event or a near miss	3.59	0.89
Board/top management	3.88	0.71

* 1 = strongly disagree; 5 = strongly agree. Std dev.: standard deviation

external drivers of risk management practices, other than competitive intensity, risk or uncertainty, were observed to be external stakeholders and the demands of regulators and legislation, enacted through boards of directors which were likely to exert influence over the policies and methods adopted for risk management.

Table 3.6   Stakeholder involvement in risk management

	Mean	*Std dev.*
Total sample		
Shareholders/analysts	2.63	1.16
Suppliers	2.66	1.04
Customers	3.16	1.08
Banks/financiers	3.04	1.08
CIMA		
Shareholders/analysts	2.60	1.16
Suppliers	2.66	1.01
Customers	3.18	1.06
Banks/financiers	3.03	1.08
FTSE		
Shareholders/analysts	2.65	1.10
Suppliers	2.65	1.16
Customers	3.00	1.10
Banks/financiers	3.10	1.08
SME		
Shareholders/analysts	2.78	1.24
Suppliers	2.63	1.11
Customers	3.22	1.15
Banks/financiers	3.03	1.10

*   1 = strongly disagree;   5 = strongly agree. Std dev.: standard
deviation

Risk propensity

Respondents were asked to identify their own propensity to take
risks and their organisation's propensity to take risks. The results
are shown in Table 3.7 (Appendix 2 contains expanded statistics
for this table).

Respondents were also asked about the extent to which this propensity had changed over the last two years. The results are shown in
Table 3.8 (Appendix 2 contains expanded statistics for this table).

Personal risk propensity was analysed by demographic characteristics using the Chi-square test. There were no statistically significant associations between risk propensity (risk averse, risk neutral
and risk willing) and organisation type, sector or size. Correlations
between personal views and the organisational approach of risk
taking and risk management are shown in Table 3.9. As would be

Table 3.7   Propensity to take risks

	*Mean	Std dev.
Total sample		
Personal propensity to take risks	3.14	0.90
Organisational propensity to take risks	3.03	0.95
CIMA		
Personal propensity to take risks	3.02	0.92
Organisational propensity to take risks	2.92	0.95
FTSE		
Personal propensity to take risks	3.56	0.70
Organisational propensity to take risks	3.42	0.91
SME		
Personal propensity to take risks	3.32	0.85
Organisational propensity to take risks	3.17	0.89

* 1 = refuse to take risks; 5 = keen to take risks. Std dev.: standard deviation

Table 3.8 Changing propensity to take risks

	*Mean	Std dev.
Total sample		
Change in personal propensity to take risks in the last 2 years	3.06	0.82
Change in organisational propensity in the last 2 years	3.14	0.87
CIMA		
Change in personal propensity to take risks in the last 2 years	3.13	0.82
Change in organisational propensity in the last 2 years	3.19	0.86
FTSE		
Change in personal propensity to take risks in the last 2 years	2.86	0.76
Change in organisational propensity in the last 2 years	2.88	0.77
SME		
Change in personal propensity to take risks in the last 2 years	2.90	0.83
Change in organisational propensity in the last 2 years	3.17	0.97

* 1 = reduced significantly; 5 = increased significantly. Std dev.: standard deviation

Table 3.9 Personal propensity versus the organisation's propensity

	CIMA	FTSE	SME	Total
Relationship between personal propensity to take risk and the organisation's propensity to take risk	0.210**	0.460**	0.702**	0.332**

** Correlation is significant at the 0.01 level (2-tailed).

expected, the personal risk propensity variable and the organisational risk propensity variable were positively correlated (0.33**). However, there was a marked difference between the samples suggesting that the fit between personal propensity and organisational propensity was not as strong for CIMA members (0.21**), as compared to SME (0.702**) and FTSE (0.460**).

Attitudes to risk

Respondents were asked the extent to which they believed that risk management was about avoiding negative consequences and achieving positive consequences. Responses to both questions were combined to compare personal and organisational risk stances. The results are shown in Tables 3.10 and 3.11.

While 73 per cent of respondents agreed that risk management was about avoiding negative consequences, 67 per cent believed it was about achieving positive ones, and 48 per cent of responses agreed that risk management was both about achieving positive consequences and avoiding negative ones. The respondents viewed their

Table 3.10 Personal perspectives about risk management (%)

		Risk management is about achieving positive consequences			
		Disagree	Neutral	Agree	Total
	Disagree	2	1	11	14
Risk management is about	Neutral	1	3	8	12
avoiding negative consequences	Agree	10	15	48	73
	Total	13	19	67	100

Table 3.11 Risk management in the organisation (%)

		Risk management is about achieving positive consequences			
		Disagree	Neutral	Agree	Total
	Disagree	1	1	5	7
Risk management is about	Neutral	0	5	9	14
avoiding negative consequences	Agree	14	22	43	79
	Total	15	28	57	100

organisations as more concerned with avoiding negative consequences (79 per cent) than about achieving positive ones (57 per
cent) with 43 per cent responding that it was about both in their
organisations.

The stance towards risk was considered, both individually and
organisationally, as an important determinant of risk management.
Risk was seen on an individual level as much about achieving positive consequences as avoiding negative ones. However, organisational risk management was more about avoiding negative
consequences. This suggests, at the organisational level, risk management was rather more likely to be about a defensive orientation
than an opportunistic one.

Risk processes and culture

Respondents were asked about the extent to which they agreed
with whether or not the organisation had a range of processes and
culture to support risk management and internal control. The
results are shown in Table 3.12 (Appendix 2 contains expanded
statistics for this table).

Overall, these responses suggest that more than half of respondents
were satisfied with their risk management processes and internal
control systems but weaker responses suggested that only about
half of respondents' organisations felt that risks were understood
and embedded at the cultural level. The results also suggest that
CIMA respondents were less confident in the formal control systems and, surprisingly, that SME responses suggest a higher degree
of formality of controls than might have been expected.

Eighty-three per cent of respondents agreed that risk should be
managed through a formal control system, but only 62 per cent
said it was managed formally in their organisations. Twenty-one
per cent of respondents agreed that it should be more a matter of
personal judgement, 25 per cent saying that this was how risk was
managed in their organisations. This has implications for informal, intuitive risk management processes. It suggests a heuristic
method of risk management is at work in contrast to the systems-
based approach that is associated with risk management in the
professional literature.

Table 3.12 Supporting processes and culture

	*Mean	Std dev.
Total sample		
Your organisation has an effective risk management policy	3.50	0.90
Risks are well understood throughout your organisation	3.32	0.90
Controlling risk is highly centralised within your organisation	3.21	1.04
Your organisation regularly reviews internal controls	3.76	0.83
Risk management is embedded in your organisation's culture	3.23	1.00
Formal procedures are in place for reporting risks	3.51	0.95
The level of internal control is appropriate for the risks faced	3.47	0.84
Your organisation is effective at prioritising risks	3.27	0.86
Changes to risks are assessed and reported on an ongoing basis	3.41	0.92
CIMA		
Your organisation has an effective risk management policy	3.42	0.92
Risks are well understood throughout your organisation	3.25	0.94
Controlling risk is highly centralised within your organisation	3.31	0.99
Your organisation regularly reviews internal controls	3.72	0.88
Risk management is embedded in your organisation's culture	3.20	1.01
Formal procedures are in place for reporting risks	3.43	0.99
The level of internal control is appropriate for the risks faced	3.38	0.86
Your organisation is effective at prioritising risks	3.18	0.87
Changes to risks are assessed and reported on an ongoing basis	3.31	0.93
FTSE		
Your organisation has an effective risk management policy	3.86	0.79
Risks are well understood throughout your organisation	3.51	0.77
Controlling risk is highly centralised within your organisation	2.80	1.15
Your organisation regularly reviews internal controls	3.96	0.50
Risk management is embedded in your organisation's culture	3.37	0.95
Formal procedures are in place for reporting risks	3.82	0.73
The level of internal control is appropriate for the risks faced	3.65	0.66
Your organisation is effective at prioritising risks	3.45	0.79
Changes to risks are assessed and reported on an ongoing basis	3.69	0.87
SME		
Your organisation has an effective risk management policy	3.51	0.78
Risks are well understood throughout your organisation	3.51	0.71
Controlling risk is highly centralised within your organisation	3.10	1.07
Your organisation regularly reviews internal controls	3.78	0.85
Risk management is embedded in your organisation's culture	3.24	0.97
Formal procedures are in place for reporting risks	3.59	0.87
The level of internal control is appropriate for the risks faced	3.78	0.79
Your organisation is effective at prioritising risks	3.59	0.74
Changes to risks are assessed and reported on an ongoing basis	3.63	0.86

* 1 = strongly disagree; 5 = strongly agree. Std dev.: standard deviation

The correlations in Table 3.3 reveal strong relationships between:

1. supporting processes and culture and the usage of basic and technical methods of risk management
2. risks being factored into plans and improved performance and external relationships
3. stakeholder involvement and risks being factored into plans, improving performance and external relationships
4. the use of various methods of risk management and risks being factored into plans, improved performance and external relationships.

Trends in risk management approach

Respondents indicated whether risk was not considered, considered tacitly, but not documented or formally managed, considered and formally documented in a systematic way, or considered, documented and used to aid decision-making, all in relation to three time periods – two years ago, currently, and the planned approach in the next two years.

The responses to the approach to risk in the past, present and future are summarised in Figure 3.3. This reflects the respondents' experience that risk has shifted from being considered tacitly to being considered more formally and their expectation that this trend will shift markedly to a more holistic approach with risk being used to aid decision-making.

A trend in risk management observed was from risk being considered tacitly in the past to it being considered formally in the present,

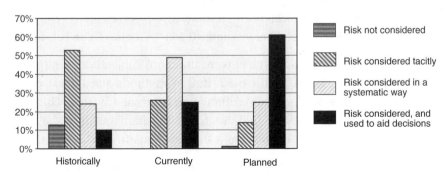

Figure 3.3 Trends in risk management

together with the expectation that in the future there would be a more holistic approach to risk being used to aid decision-making. This may be a reasonable expectation, an aspiration or it may reflect some unease in our respondents that risk management practices in use do not appear to connect to organisation or business problems or contribute as much to decision-making as they consider necessary or desirable. If the latter is so then the picture may represent a somewhat idealised picture, which may continue to exist.

Although the FTSE group saw their current approach as largely formal compared to the other survey groups, and the SME group reflected a lower degree of formality expected in the future, all survey groups (including CIMA) reflected a similar trend to that shown in Figure 3.3. There was also a stronger view by CIMA respondents that risk was considered systematically and used in decision-making than that of FTSE who see it as largely tacit. There was a similarity in the expected shift by both CIMA and FTSE respondents from divergent positions historically and currently to a consistent planned approach in which risk is systematically considered rather than tacit and largely used to aid decision-making.

Risk management methods

We separated the risk management methods used into two categories: basic and technical. These are shown in Table 3.13.

The usage rates of these risk management methods are shown in Table 3.14 (Appendix 2 contains expanded statistics for this table). Table 3.3 showed that the only correlations of the external environmental uncertainty were with the Effectiveness of technical methods for the whole sample (0.14*) and the CIMA subsample (0.14*). However, environmental uncertainty correlated with the Effectiveness of technical methods (0.454**) for the FTSE subsample.

The methods in highest use were the more subjective ones (particularly experience), with quantitative methods used least of all. There was also significant reliance on external advisers. This reinforces the conjecture that heuristic mechanisms may be more important for risk management than systematic mechanisms.

The degree to which these methods were observed to be effective in helping respondents' organisations to manage risk was highly

Table 3.13 Categories of risk management methods

Basic methods of risk management	Technical methods of risk management
◆ Brainstorming, scenario analysis, PEST/SWOT analysis ◆ Interviews, surveys, questionnaires ◆ Likelihood/consequences matrix ◆ Monitoring using a risk register or written reports	◆ Stochastic modelling, statistical analysis ◆ Risk management software

Table 3.14 Usage rate of risk management methods

	*Mean	Std dev.
Total sample		
Usage rate of basic methods	2.76	0.87
Usage rate of technical methods	1.91	0.99
Use of experience, intuition, hindsight, judgement to management risk	3.89	0.89
Use of auditors or external consultants to management risk	2.91	1.23
CIMA		
Usage rate of basic methods	2.72	0.89
Usage rate of technical methods	2.02	1.03
Use of experience, intuition, hindsight, judgement to management risk	3.87	0.86
Use of auditors or external consultants to management risk	2.99	1.28
FTSE		
Usage rate of basic methods	2.83	0.84
Usage rate of technical methods	3.04	0.78
Use of experience, intuition, hindsight, judgement to management risk	3.92	1.00
Use of auditors or external consultants to management risk	2.63	1.01
SME		
Usage rate of basic methods	2.90	0.81
Usage rate of technical methods	2.70	0.85
Use of experience, intuition, hindsight, judgement to management risk	3.95	0.95
Use of auditors or external consultants to management risk	2.78	1.19

* 1 = low; 5 = high. Std dev.: standard deviation

correlated with the degree of use, as might be expected. If a method was not perceived as effective it was unlikely to continue in use. An exception was that there was less confidence in experience, intuition, hindsight and judgement with only 48 per cent of respondents believing that these were the most effective methods, compared with the 70 per cent of respondents who used that method.

Table 3.3 (total sample) reveals that there were strong relationships between supporting processes and culture and the usage of basic and technical methods of risk management, risks being factored into plans and improved performance and external relationships.

However, a higher proportion of FTSE and SME respondents believed that risk management in their organisations was handled through a formal control system, reinforcing the suggestion that CIMA respondents may have had less confidence than other respondents in the use of control systems for risk management purposes.

Involvement of accountants in risk management

Those reported to be primarily accountable for the processes of identifying risk, analysing and assessing risk, deciding on risk management action, and reporting and monitoring risk are shown in Table 3.15.

Deciding on risk management action was predominantly the concern of the chief executive and the board. Finance directors had a major role in analysing and assessing, and reporting and monitoring risk. The finance director was identified with more aspects of risk management than any other role, suggesting that they may have a pivotal role in risk management. The responses reveal that line managers were mostly concerned with identifying risk, analysing and reporting on risk.

Management accountants were scored lower than internal audit and risk managers on the identification of risk. They were equal with internal auditors but lower than risk managers on analysing and assessing risk. They were lower than internal auditors and risk managers in deciding on risk management action and only scored slightly higher than internal auditors in reporting and monitoring risk.

Table 3.15 Job title primarily accountable for risk management

	Identifying risks		Analysing assessing risks		Deciding on risk management action		Reporting monitoring risk	
	Count	%	Count	%	Count	%	Count	%
CEO/managing director	83	15	44	9	121	25	33	7
Board/audit committee	65	12	59	12	126	26	57	12
Director of finance	72	13	87	18	97	20	86	19
Internal audit	55	10	63	13	23	5	60	13
Risk manager	70	13	79	16	42	9	76	16
Management accountant	45	8	63	13	12	2	63	14
Line managers	155	28	87	18	64	13	86	19
Total count	**545**	**100**	**482**	**100**	**485**	**100**	**461**	**100**

Table 3.16 Integration of organisational management accounting and risk management functions

	*Mean	Std dev.
Total sample	2.81	0.97
CIMA	2.81	0.97

* 1 = strongly disagree; 5 = strongly agree. Std dev.: standard deviation

The extent to which management accounting and risk management were reported to be integrated in organisations is given in Table 3.16 (Appendix 2 contains expanded statistics for this table).

CIMA respondents were also asked whether, in terms of risk management, their level of involvement of management accounting was sufficient. The results are shown in Table 3.17.

There was little reported integration between management accounting and risk management, and management accountants in the overwhelming majority of organisations were being marginalised in relation to risk management. While CIMA respondents feel that

Table 3.17 The level of involvement of management accounting in the organisation's risk management

	Insufficient (%)	About right (%)	Too involved (%)	No view (%)
Total sample	37	57	2	4
CIMA	37	57	2	4
FTSE	10	80	6	4
SME	20	76	2	2

	Increasing (%)	Not changing (%)	Decreasing (%)	No view (%)
Total sample	42	50	3	5
CIMA	43	48	4	5
FTSE	33	61	0	7
SME	47	50	0	3

management accountants should have more involvement in risk management, this was not a view shared by other respondents.

Perceived consequences of risk management

The reported degrees of improvement brought about as a consequence of risk management are shown in Table 3.18 (Appendix 2 contains expanded statistics for this table).

Responses were fairly evenly spread, although more respondents believed there had been no improvement in relations with shareholders and suppliers, while management reporting and reputation had improved the most.

The extent to which various choices were made in risk management and the reported effectiveness of those choices is shown in Tables 3.19 and 3.20 (Appendix 2 contains expanded statistics for these tables).

Modes of risk management

Although all methods were in high use, management action to decrease the likelihood of risk was given the highest ranking. The

Table 3.18 Consequences of risk management

	*Mean	Std dev.
Total sample		
RM has improved corporate planning	2.85	0.91
RM has improved resource allocation and utilisation	2.83	0.96
RM has improved management reporting	3.05	1.02
RM has improved communication within the organisation	2.77	1.02
RM has improved relationships with shareholders	2.34	1.08
RM has improved relationships with customers/clients	2.70	1.01
RM has improved relationships with suppliers	2.44	1.02
RM has improved management of organisational change	2.91	0.99
RM has improved reputation	2.92	1.08
RM has improved recognition and uptake of opportunities	2.88	1.02
RM has improved employee confidence in carrying out their duties	2.69	0.99
CIMA		
RM has improved corporate planning	2.78	0.92
RM has improved resource allocation and utilisation	2.81	0.96
RM has improved management reporting	2.94	1.02
RM has improved communication within the organisation	2.68	1.01
RM has improved relationships with shareholders	2.36	1.08
RM has improved relationships with customers/clients	2.70	1.01
RM has improved relationships with suppliers	2.46	1.02
RM has improved management of organisational change	2.83	1.00
RM has improved reputation	2.86	1.06
RM has improved recognition and uptake of opportunities	2.85	1.00
RM has improved employee confidence in carrying out their duties	2.64	1.01
FTSE		
RM has improved corporate planning	3.04	0.83
RM has improved resource allocation and utilisation	2.84	0.98
RM has improved management reporting	3.22	1.06
RM has improved communication within the organisation	2.73	1.02
RM has improved relationships with shareholders	2.32	1.12
RM has improved relationships with customers/clients	2.50	1.07
RM has improved relationships with suppliers	2.26	1.07
RM has improved management of organisational change	3.00	0.99
RM has improved reputation	2.82	1.10
RM has improved recognition and uptake of opportunities	2.82	1.12
RM has improved employee confidence in carrying out their duties	2.64	0.85
SME		
RM has improved corporate planning	2.95	0.93
RM has improved resource allocation and utilisation	2.90	0.93

(Continued)

Table 3.18 (*Continued*)

	*Mean	Std dev.
RM has improved management reporting	3.48	0.88
RM has improved communication within the organisation	3.30	0.99
RM has improved relationships with shareholders	2.26	1.00
RM has improved relationships with customers/clients	2.98	0.95
RM has improved relationships with suppliers	2.55	0.93
RM has improved management of organisational change	3.25	0.84
RM has improved reputation	3.35	1.05
RM has improved recognition and uptake of opportunities	3.15	1.03
RM has improved employee confidence in carrying out their duties	3.05	0.96

* 1 = no improvement; 5 = significant improvement. Std dev.: standard deviation

Table 3.19 Risk management options employed

	*Mean	Std dev.
Total sample		
Transferring the risk using insurance, hedging, contracts, joint ventures or partnerships, etc.	3.09	1.25
Decreasing the likelihood of risk through management action	3.61	0.93
Decreasing adverse consequences of risk using contingency, business continuity plans, etc.	3.25	1.02
CIMA		
Transferring the risk using insurance, hedging, contracts, joint ventures or partnerships, etc.	2.98	1.29
Decreasing the likelihood of risk through management action	3.53	0.96
Decreasing adverse consequences of risk using contingency, business continuity plans, etc.	3.20	1.07
FTSE		
Transferring the risk using insurance, hedging, contracts, joint ventures or partnerships, etc.	3.66	1.02
Decreasing the likelihood of risk through management action	3.90	0.76
Decreasing adverse consequences of risk using contingency, business continuity plans, etc.	3.46	0.86
SME		
Transferring the risk using insurance, hedging, contracts, joint ventures or partnerships, etc.	3.05	1.07
Decreasing the likelihood of risk through management action	3.76	0.83
Decreasing adverse consequences of risk using contingency, business continuity plans, etc.	3.24	0.83

* 1 = low; 5 = high. Std dev.: standard deviation

Table 3.20 Perceived effectiveness of risk management approaches

	*Mean	Std dev.
Total sample		
Effectiveness of transferring risk	3.08	1.22
Effectiveness of decreasing the likelihood of risk	3.48	0.94
Effectiveness of decreasing adverse consequences	3.14	1.02
CIMA		
Effectiveness of transferring risk	3.00	1.26
Effectiveness of decreasing the likelihood of risk	3.41	0.93
Effectiveness of decreasing adverse consequences	3.09	1.05
FTSE		
Effectiveness of transferring risk	3.45	1.12
Effectiveness of decreasing the likelihood of risk	3.84	0.87
Effectiveness of decreasing adverse consequences	3.42	0.91
SME		
Effectiveness of transferring risk	3.10	1.03
Effectiveness of decreasing the likelihood of risk	3.50	0.99
Effectiveness of decreasing adverse consequences	3.13	0.97

* 1 = low; 5 = high. Std dev.: standard deviation

responses imply that traditional methods of managing risk through transfer (insurance, hedging, etc.) were still seen as more effective than more proactive risk management processes.

CIMA responses were slightly more sceptical about the benefits to corporate planning, management reporting and the management of organisational change but were more convinced than FTSE (but less than SME) of the improvements in relationships with customers/clients and of employee confidence in carrying out their duties. FTSE was slightly higher in their belief that relationships with shareholders had improved.

Costs and benefits of risk management

The extent to which respondents agreed that risk management practices had delivered benefits that exceeded the cost of the practices is shown in Table 3.21.

While risk management was perceived to be costlier than the benefits by a tenth of respondents, 50 per cent believe the benefits exceed the costs. Given the major publicity and governance requirements,

Table 3.21 RM practices have delivered benefits that exceed the costs of those practices

	*Mean	Std dev.
Total sample	3.45	0.81
CIMA	3.41	0.81
FTSE	3.56	0.93
SME	3.58	0.64

* 1 = strongly disagree; 5 = strongly agree. Std dev.: standard deviation

this suggests that risk management may be substantially seen as a (costly) compliance exercise. However, half of the respondents reported that the benefits exceeded the costs which, taken together with the heuristic processes dominating the systematic processes, might imply that the costs of risk management differs widely across the respondents' organisations.

Risk stance

Using the ideal types applied to risk management developed in Figure 1.1 and based on the work of Douglas and Wildavsky (1983) and Adams (1995), we categorised the response about risk management in the respondent's organisation being about positive/negative consequences in Figure 3.4.

The correlations above were calculated for each group of organisations in the four stances. These differences, although not great, do lend support to the distinction between fatalists (or risk sceptical), hierarchists, individualists, and egalitarians (or risk aware). We therefore considered that the risk stance of managers did influence the risk management practices in use.

Regression analysis

The strong correlations and differences reported in the grouped variables between the types of respondents and their risk stances suggested that the working hypothesis that risk management leads to improvement could be further explored. First, the hypothesis was examined using linear regression expressing improved performance as a function of the other group variables for all of the data set.

RM is about achieving positive consequences in my organisation

		Disagree	Neutral	Agree
RM is about avoiding negative consequences in my organisation	**Disagree**	Risk sceptical 7%		Entrepreneurs 14%
	Neutral			
	Agree	Hierarchists 36%		Risk aware 43%

Figure 3.4 Classification of risk management responses by risk stance

The variables Effectiveness of basic methods and Effectiveness of technical methods were not included in the regressions because of their almost universal high correlations with their usage variables. The regression equations with all of the variables were found to produce high adjusted R squared, but the statistical significance of the variable coefficients were low. The variables relating the degree of uncertainty of the external environment, stakeholder involvement and the effectiveness of technical methods always had coefficients with less then 0.05 significance levels. This pattern followed the pattern of statistical significance of the correlation matrix.

The regression equations for the whole data set are shown in Table 3.22, with the regression equation coefficients, adjusted R squared, Anova and significance levels shown. The best (in terms of significance levels of the estimators) regression for all the data included the usage variables: Use of basic methods (having a negative coefficient), the Effectiveness of basic methods, Use of technical methods, and the two process variables: Supporting policies and culture; and Risk factored into plans.

The Effectiveness of basic methods was then removed from the regression for all the data to test the shift in adjusted R squared. There was little effect (Table 3.22), but the Use of basic methods was not significant. Removing the Use of basic methods variable from the regression then gave a three variable equation with high statistical significance to the variable coefficients and an R squared of 0.44. The equation has surprisingly strong predictive power. It also provides some support for the findings from the case studies that how risk is taken into the processes of planning may be more important than the actual methods used.

The exploration of the regression for the four identified risk stance sets of data is given in Table 3.23. The regression equations were

Table 3.22 Improved performance: linear regressions for group variables

Category	Constant	Use of basic methods	Effectiveness of basic methods	Use of technical methods	Supporting policies and culture	Risk factored into plans	Adjusted R squared	ANOVA Significance
All data	3.61*	-0.452***	0.654***	0.479***	0.381***	0.417***	0.45	***
	3.37*	0.174		0.456**	0.364***	0.460***	0.45	***
	3.72*			0.569***	0.405***	0.463***	0.44	***
Risk sceptical	-5.06	-0.244		0.466	0.683*	0.799	0.54	*
	-5.44				0.670*	0.792*	0.58	**
Hierarchist	-0.613	0.369**		0.693**	0.371***	0.418***	0.54	***
Entrepreneur	16.4**	0.143		0.852	0.083	0.261	0.16	*
	18.4***			1.030*		0.317	0.20	**
Risk aware	7.6**	0.015		0.314	0.337***	0.442***	0.35	***
	7.43**				0.382***	0.466***	0.36	***

Significance levels: * 0.05, **0.01, *** 0.001. Blank indicates that variable was not included.

Table 3.23 Risk stance: predictor variables and adjusted R squared

	Degree to which risk is about protection	
Degree to which risk is about exploiting opportunities	*Risk sceptical* 2 process variables 0.56	*Hierarchist* 2 usage variables 2 process variables 0.54
	Entrepreneur 1 usage variable 0.20	*Risk aware* 2 process variables 0.36

stronger predictors (higher R squared) when the risk stance was not about exploiting opportunities – hierarchist and risk sceptical. It was best fitted to the model for the hierarchist case, with the regression including the two usage variables and the two process variables and a high adjusted R squared of 0.54. When risk stance was entrepreneur, about exploiting opportunities, then only one variable appeared (Use of technical methods), but the adjusted R squared was low at 0.20. For the risk aware case only two variables entered the regression, both were process oriented, with an adjusted R squared of 0.36.

These results suggest that risk stance was a significant moderating influence on methods of risk management and these then led to reported improved performance of these firms. The two process variables – Supporting policies and culture, and Risk factored into plans – were clearly of great interest. From the questionnaire design, it is difficult to state with confidence that the significance and full meaning of these have been captured. It suggests that our respondents, while able to answer the questions asked, were also aware of different kinds of processes in which risk was being managed. Perhaps the initial hypothesis and the variables chosen were more closely related to risk management from the stance of the idea of risk as being not about opportunity but being about protection for that was where the model had its best fit. This observation implies that risk management is mostly conceived of as fitting a hierarchist stance in respect of methods and a process stance in respect of the risk aware firms.

Risk management and financial market risk

It was open to the respondents to identify themselves or their organisations as they thought appropriate. From the 333 responses it was possible to draw a further smaller sample of identified

Table 3.24 Mean values of risk measures in relation to risk
stance

Stance	Beta	Alpha	Volatility
Total	0.98	0.0022	28.72
Risk sceptical	1.16	0.0002	20.67
Hierarchist	1.06	0.004	27.10
Entrepreneur	1.14	0.0006	40.32
Risk aware	0.82	0.002	25.72

quoted companies (n=41). From the respondents' voluntary disclosure of their organisation it was possible to explore the degree to which reported risk management practices were related to capital market views of these organisations to see whether risk management practices increased, was neutral to or decreased *beta*, *alpha* and volatility. The results are shown in Table 3.24.

The sample value of *beta* 0.98 indicates that the sample of 41 companies was close to a reasonable sample of the market. Also the volatility in each class was very similar. Interestingly, the *alpha* value for the hierarchist group was the highest, perhaps suggesting that given risk stance, then risk protection might provide higher performance. Further, it was found that the *beta* values correlated at 0.393 (P= 0.011) with the variable Change in uncertainty and correlated at [m]0.558 (P=0.01) with the variable Risks factored into plans.

The regression equations of improved performance from this small sample were similar to the earlier equations for the whole sample, with an adjusted R squared of 0.57. The regression included the same four variables but the coefficient of the Use of basic methods was negative.

Hence, it may be observed that there is an indication that the market *beta* for the risk aware group was lower than that for the other groups. A Chi-squared test on the four stances revealed that, because of the small numbers in each cell, the differences between the values in the four cells were not statistically significant. However, collapsing the data into two sets, risk aware and all others, gave differences in *beta* which were not significant at the 0.05 level.

The implication of these observations is that the risk aware stance, in attending to both protection and to opportunity, may affect organisations through the capital markets award of a lower *beta*, and hence a higher market value. Here it may be inferred that the requirements of corporate governance do not necessarily have to work in opposition to economic rationales of risk as opportunity and adventure. Given the small sample, this observation should be treated as indicative rather than definitive and this part of the study needs to be replicated on a much larger scale. However, these indications offer a somewhat tantalising glimpse of the possible inter-relationship of market, cultural, economic and governance rationales for risk management.

Summary of main survey findings

Contrary to expectations that risk management practices vary between organisations as a result of their size or industry sector, there was little evidence of any contingent explanations for risk management based on either size or business sector. Similarly, if somewhat surprisingly, respondents' perceptions of the environmental uncertainty and risk facing their organisations did not appear to influence basic risk management practices in those organisations, but did, in the case of the FTSE companies, influence the use of technical methods.

However, perhaps reinforcing traditional stereotypes, CIMA respondents were more risk-concerned than the other respondent groups in relation to their organisations, despite having a lower perception of the competitive intensity and uncertainty in their industry/sector.

The survey results suggested that risk management was driven by an institutional response to calls for improved corporate governance which may reflect both protection and economic opportunity. The external drivers of risk management practices, rather than competitive intensity, risk or uncertainty, were observed to be external stakeholders and the demands of regulators and legislation, enacted through boards of directors, which were likely to exert influence over the policies and methods adopted for risk management.

However, the trends in risk management were reported to have shifted from being considered tacitly to being considered more formally and the survey results reflected the respondents' expectation that this trend will shift markedly to a more holistic approach with risk management being used to aid decision-making.

Risk was seen on an individual level as much about achieving positive consequences as avoiding negative ones. However, organisational risk management was reported to be more about avoiding negative consequences.

The survey found that the methods for risk management that were in highest use were the more subjective ones (particularly experience), with quantitative methods used least of all, a result which replicates many studies. There was also significant reliance on external advisers. These results suggested a heuristic method of risk management is at work in contrast to the systems-based approach that is associated with risk management in much professional training and in the professional literature.

The reliance on formal accounting-based controls was also called into question. Importantly, CIMA respondents were less confident in the formal control systems that existed in their organisations, suggesting that the professional knowledge of accountants accommodates an understanding of the limits of accounting information, a knowledge not shared by non-accountants.

This research has some significant and important implications for the role of accountants. The responses reveal that line managers were mostly concerned with identifying risk, analysing and reporting on risk. Finance directors had a major role in analysing and assessing, and reporting and monitoring risk. Deciding on risk management action was predominantly the concern of the chief executive and the board. Management accountants were scored lower than internal audit and risk managers on the identification of risk. The finance director was identified with more aspects of risk management than any other role, suggesting that they probably have a pivotal role in risk management.

There was little reported integration between management accounting and risk management. Further, management accountants in the overwhelming majority of organisations were being marginalised in relation to risk management. While CIMA respondents consider that management accountants should have more involvement in risk management, this was not a view shared by other respondents.

Given the major role of public visibility of governance requirements, risk management may be seen largely as a compliance exercise. However, half of the respondents reported that the benefits exceeded the costs, with 40 per cent reporting that benefits and costs were neutral. Perhaps unsurprisingly, from a risk averse standpoint, management action to decrease the likelihood of risk was given the highest ranking, rather than action to achieve organisational objectives. The survey responses implied that traditional methods of managing risk through transfer (insurance, hedging, etc.) were still seen as more effective than more proactive risk management processes.

In relation to financial market risk, the implication of our regression analysis is that the risk aware stance, in attending to both protection and to opportunity, does create organisations to which the capital markets award a lower *beta*, and hence a higher value. This led us to infer that the requirements of corporate governance do not necessarily have to work in opposition to economic rationales of risk as opportunity and adventure. However, given the small samples, this observation is indicative only and would need to be replicated on a larger scale.

Interview data

To help us to interpret some of the findings in the analysis of our survey results, we conducted interviews with 14 members of organizations who had indicated in their survey questionnaires that they were prepared to be interviewed. Ten were interviewed face to face and four by telephone. The interviews were based on semi-structured, open questions in order not to lead the respondents. Transcripts of the interviews were made for later analysis. This section is based upon excerpts from these interviews, in order to explore the key issues emerging from the survey.

The traditional approach to risk management

Four organizations we interviewed perhaps best describe the traditional approach to risk management.

We spoke to the commercial director of the conference organizing subsidiary of a multinational NASDAQ-listed advertising group who described risk in his organization.

> Risk is the ability to meet annual sales, gross profit and net profit forecasts. But there is a gap between the actual committed business on the books and the forecast which comes from pressure from the analysts to achieve a particular share price, hence our parent is now a takeover target.

The business risk is not only having insufficient business, but winning business that stretches the available resources as events may have to be staged at the same time to meet client demands.

> We are only as good as our last event. This lies with our project directors at the point of delivery. Any difference of opinion with the client has the potential to be our last event. The risk of having a single point of contact in a client is that if that person moves on it is more of a risk than an opportunity.

Risk is not an agenda item on management meetings, even though the business aspires to double in size over the next three years.

> The risk is that we can either win business then recruit up, or recruit in anticipation of winning business. We default to the more conservative.

The business is conservative. The group's key performance measures are based on tight control of overheads and margins. This means we are less likely to take considered or managed risk, although this is sometimes betrayed by particular clients or projects.

An account director for the same organization added:

I think it will change. We are following the US with litigation. There is more pressure to demonstrate the ability to manage risk, especially where we are working in public spaces.

The general manager and supply chain director for an aerospace division of a management buyout funded by institutional investors replied:

There is no structured approach to identify risks. There is an annual budget, a quarterly board review and a monthly rolling forecast. I consider risk as part of forecasting. The finance director keeps contingencies and provisions to manage the financial risk. There is a large burden of interest charges as a result of the institutional buy-out. We are caught between big suppliers and big customers. If we don't pay the supplier stops credit, but we don't stop the customer's credit when they don't pay on time.

If we introduce new parts there is project management, and risk management takes place through failure mode and effect analysis (FMEA).

Risks are not well understood in this company.

We are totally reactive. We are obsessed with day-to-day production. We are starting to look at preventive maintenance but we need headroom and resources to do that.

Two examples served to illustrate this reactivity.

We had a 12 000 tonne press that was the largest in Europe, having been bought 50 years previously. A 25 tonne piece of steel cracked. The risk of this happening was low, it had been there for 20 years with no problem. It could be argued that we should have had a spare or a routine inspection programme but we hadn't got that level of detail. The result was that the press was down for a week and we lost a quarter of the month's production and delays to projects, which in aerospace can be critical. But the mean time between failures was 20 years.

We have had 3 fires in the 14 months I have been here. There was old wiring and our risk management was that the site is next to a fire station. We have since done a complete rewiring.

The third organization was a voluntary charity, where we spoke with the vice chair, the manager and a trustee.

Risk management is not one of our strengths, we have focused on the finance issues … We ought to be looking at policy review and those sort of more managerial issues, and in there I would lump risk management … If we focus slightly narrowly on definitions of risk and how we look at that we perhaps wouldn't get too many marks out of ten.

Vice Chair

Our motivation was that it is actually the trustees or the board who have responsibility if things go wrong. Before we became a company limited by guarantee, the trustees were individually liable.

Manager

If you look at a board agenda and minutes and try to find the word risk you will struggle, but it is inherent in everything we do. I don't want to focus too much on finance, but if we use finance as an example because it's been such a big issue in the last few months, if we looked at the performance of any one area in financial terms, if it was starting to overspend we would very rapidly be aware of that and would understand the risks to the organization if we allowed that to continue … Certainly, if we ever faced a court it would be incumbent on us to show that we had actually thought about risk and done something about it.

Vice Chair

Organization four was a privately owned large engineering consultancy with 3500 employees. It had recently appointed a risk manager to address professional indemnity claims experience that had resulted in an increase in its excess per claim from £5000 to £500 000 and an annual premium of several million pounds. The company had also estimated the cost of project over-runs, non-productive time, and contractual penalties as 2 per cent of its turnover. The company had determined to increase dramatically its attention to risk management by top management leadership, management training, and greater attention to contractual negotiations and contract monitoring.

Explanations for survey results

Drivers of risk management

The survey found that the main drivers of risk management were compliance rather than competitive intensity or environmental uncertainty and we sought to explore this issue in depth with our interview respondents.

> Investment funds are driving the risk management agenda, asking questions of the board about the sustainability and reduction in volatility of profits. Turnbull raised understanding of the issue but a few were taking issue before Turnbull, although most came after.
>
> *Chief Executive, UK association of risk managers*

> Stakeholders are starting to ask more questions on how you run your business and so forth. The media is obviously another one, so the knowledge within the market is becoming greater, therefore there is a need for greater transparency. I believe we are developing our **risk** process on the need to demonstrate transparency ... I think historically risks have been hidden. Whereas if you actually say, look at these risks I have identified, this is how I am managing it, I think people are more impressed because you've thought about it, you know what is coming up, and you are putting something in place to manage it.
>
> *Group Risk Manager, FTSE company, Financial Services*

> The drivers were all Turnbull really, we are obliged to take it seriously, so that was the driver. It's a combination of Turnbull, Health and Safety together with some insurance stipulations.
>
> *Finance Director, subsidiary of listed PLC*

An alternative view was expressed by SMEs, whose focus was more direct.

> I think the biggest driver is profit. We are constantly looking at how we can improve the profitability of this company and that will throw up various things that we need to do which will, of course, incur ever increasing risks. Whatever decision, expanding, contracting, it still incurs risks that we have to try and deal with.
>
> *Chairman, SME, computer retail*

However, business shocks also featured as an important instigator of risk management activity.

To be honest, about 10 years ago we had a disastrous project. After that we had to have a hard look at the way we did things. Main board were insisting that we adopt more rigorous procedures. That was the main driver for risk management really.

Non-executive director, SME, Contracting

The motivation for risk management is to establish best practice in corporate governance in case we need to float [on the stock exchange] again. We did have problems recently with our fundamental controls when senior managers were looking at takeovers and refinancing and took their eye off the ball.

Group audit manager of an unquoted retail company with
around 500 retail stores, a CIMA member, with
responsibility for risk management, referring to high
profile news stories a year or two earlier

But there was one respondent who, perhaps, was more honest than he needed to be. The same group audit manager described in detail for us the role of the risk management committee, the brainstorming of 'risk drivers', the production of a risk register, determining controls and the effectiveness of controls, visual risk maps that show both the probability and severity of risk (quantified in monetary terms), and the separation and reporting of gross risk (before implementation of controls) and net or residual risk (the risk remaining after controls are implemented). However, at the end of the interview, almost as an afterthought, he added:

This looks great on paper, it gives confidence to external audit and the audit committee. There should be business benefits, but as it is, it is important. It is a political tool.

Group audit manager of an unquoted retail company,
with responsibility for risk management

The survey results suggested that the competitive environment did not seem to have much impact as a driver of risk management. Only a few respondents commented on this.

I think in the present climate that is probably true, although it is starting to change. Turnbull has been a driver to actually put it on the agenda. This year I have met with three FTSE 100 Chairmen and two FTSE 100 CEOs to talk about risk management. The broad impression I have got from them is that risk management is moving from a box-ticking exercise and the board is beginning to see the value of it, although it varies considerably within organisations. So it is beginning to change by adding some business value, but it is certainly driven by compliance.

Vice President, European federation of
risk management associations

The SME view was again focused on more immediate concerns.

The problem I am faced with right now is increasing competition and diminishing margins, which is a big risk and threat ... I've got to find ways of running with less sales people, doing more business and again it comes back to software and information that allows me to find out as much information as I can about our customers.

Chairman, SME, computer retail

Trends in risk management

The trends in risk management that the survey identified revealed a marked shift from the historic tacit consideration of risk to the current systematic approach driven by the need for compliance (which respondents repeatedly referred to as the 'tick-box' approach) and the suggestion that, in future, risk would be considered and used to make decisions (which again, was typically referred to by respondents as risk being 'culturally embedded'). We asked our respondents for their views on this shift.

The tick-box and procedures help identify the risks which are brought to us and facilitate our ability to decide how we are going to manage them.

Non-executive director, SME, Contracting

Moving beyond the tick-box approach is certainly a goal of the organisation ... We focus in on the top 10 risks, we don't just tick a box and think that we've got the procedures in place therefore we are risk free. It's identifying and ranking these in terms of importance ... the move from tick box to value adding is very much driven by guidance given by our parent company.

Finance director, subsidiary of listed PLC

The key issue is to actually do a few things that demonstrate some value from that exercise. Now most business managers are naturally focused on personal rewards and so on their business plan. When you ask them to explain their strategy and start asking questions like 'What's going to knock that off course?' they don't understand the question. They say 'We've got it all planned, we've looked at the sensitivities'. Most people do the sensitivity around a plan quite well, but it doesn't take care of the real risks. Once they see that, they start thinking outside the box and suddenly they can see some value because they can see that there are potential issues that will actually knock their plan off course [and impact their personal rewards]. What they can see from risk management is a means of trying to limit the area of unpredictability.

Vice President, European federation of
risk management associations

My belief is that there is a strong desire, certainly in my business, not just to have it as a box-ticking exercise – a very strong desire – but there is the clear recognition that it can be a box-ticking exercise and that perhaps other people, although I suspect less these days, are looking at it like that. There is a strong desire to get business value out of what we do and therefore one of the biggest challenges for me and my colleagues is to make sure what we do is of a non-bureaucratic, non-administratively rich environment, but that is certainly meeting the Code, because philosophically we do agree with the requirement and need for stronger governance structures, but we take the opportunity to strengthen the business in doing this.

Risk manager, telecommunications PLC with
UK and US listing

Effectiveness of methods

The introduction of more sophisticated risk management techniques would, we had assumed, naturally follow from a compliance-focus. However, this was not the case in the survey results. Even for FTSE respondents, only about half believed that the more technical or sophisticated methods of risk management were not particularly effective.

I think that's probably true. Keep it simple is the easiest approach. It's the most effective in terms of getting people locked into it because, if you come up with a complicated, complex process, it's yet another thing for people to learn and understand. The danger is it really tends to then continue the silo mentality of doing lots of things in business. It creates another silo of information and analysis. If it's simple, then you can embed it in the process.

Vice President, European federation of
risk management associations

I agree that it should definitely be intuition and experience. I suppose sprinkled over with a bit of objectivity, which is where the accountant comes. I don't think using software is the answer, I think you would be going back to a box-ticking exercise.

Finance Director, subsidiary of listed PLC

It is very difficult to get a solid database on which to start doing quantitative analysis you know, the world changes and all the factors change, so it is very difficult to start putting figures on. I think intuitive at the moment is certainly the move we're making ... I think it's very intuitive, in that you learn as you go along and the only way you can do that is on past experience and therefore the more experience you can tap into, the better your intuition can become ... There is a use for impact/probability because it enables you to provide a pictorial representation of where you think the risks are. Now, if you are looking at busy directors, if you give them **that** one page pictorial view, it focuses their minds. Then you get more time to discuss the risks, rather than giving them reams of paper.

Group Risk Manager, FTSE company, Financial Services

However, it was recognised that while sophisticated methods of risk management were used, these were evident at lower organisational levels, rather than at corporate level, where the methods were subjective, based on experience and intuition (in our survey results we classified these as basic).

We use sophisticated methods, but not on every job. When there is potentially a high risk, and we need better quantification we will employ a more sophisticated and analytical approach. We will write down risks and make an assessment of each risk using statistical analysis. Of course, this is still only a guide for a decision that will rely on experience and intuition as well.

Non-executive director, SME, Contracting

Most of the more sophisticated methods, although that is not quite the right word, have specialist uses which are valuable if applied in the right place, but don't tend to carry value in my view if you try and use them across a whole business. What I do and have done in previous organizations and which is well accepted by boards and is mostly seen as adding value can be described as the more touchy feely. It is around workshops, it's around risk assessment, it's around simple risk mapping and simple summaries of risk mitigation and actions out of that. That becomes a continuous process of looking at that type of thing in a simple, quick, normal management – as much as possible – style of doing things. Now that's not to say that those types of much more sophisticated techniques don't have their place – I believe that they often do – but they need to be used and valued in a much more focused environment, not business-wide.

Risk manager, telecommunications PLC
with UK and US listing

Even those who used apparently objective techniques were dubious about their reliability. One respondent demonstrated the subjectivity of figures that were the result of extensive analysis:

> Our risk map reports show that the value of the recommendations made by our risk management committee is about £268 million. This is how much the business would be better off by implementing those recommendations, although the real figure is probably only half of this.

Group audit manager of an unquoted retail company,
with responsibility for risk management

The complexity of business and the environment in which it operates was a key theme for our respondents.

> Our risk management processes are based on experience and to a certain extent gut feel ... if you go the complex route with all sorts of statistical analysis then to a certain extent, what are you adding to the business? The business knows what it is trying to achieve and it's the risks it is wanting to look at, not necessarily all of the analysis that goes with it.

Group Risk Manager, FTSE company, who also acknowledged
that they were waiting to see what the Financial
Services Authority expected of them

Involvement of management accountants in risk management

We were, of course, particularly interested in the role of management accountants, particularly when our survey highlighted that while management accountants wanted to become more involved in risk management, other organizational members did not share that view.

We asked a management accountant about this. The interview commenced with the management accountant saying he did not contribute much to risk management. But as the interview progressed, it became clear that much of what he did was risk management, he just had not realised it.

> The risk to the editor is that he would not get sufficient money to develop his circulation target contained in the five-year strategy. For example, the new [named] section was based on attracting half a million readers, but this was based on the editor's gut feel. The accountant qualifies this in a mini-business plan ... I transform the editor's gut feeling to numbers on a piece of paper.
>
> *Management accountant, broadsheet newspaper,*
> *part of multinational group*

Primarily, however, we explored this with the non-accountants.

> The accountant has an operational risk to perform and they have their own set of risks ... I think they have got quite a pivotal role, in terms of analysis and modelling, of where we are going and I am bringing actuaries into that category as well in terms of helping to quantify and assess the impact of risk ... in developing the sort of formulae that are required to make assessments.
>
> *Group Risk Manager, FTSE company,*
> *Financial Services*

> I don't think the management accountant has any more responsibility than say a production director, a commercial services director or whatever. I think in practice it's one of those legislative requirements that tend to get dumped on accountants.
>
> *Finance Director, subsidiary of listed PLC*

The predominant view was that accountants should be in supportive rather than a leading role in relation to risk management. It was generally agreed that management accountants had an important role to play, but this was largely concerned with producing analyses of impact of risks to support risk managers.

> Accountants are good at identifying qualitative issues. They carry weight because they can argue that there is a limit to numeracy. It is a challenge for the profession as only a small number of people are comfortable with change and the entrepreneurial ethos. The financial manager is often the risk manager for the organization. The risk manager may have the ear of the board, but the finance director sits on the board. Actuaries have been invisible in risk management.
>
> *Chief Executive, UK association of risk managers*

Management accountants are the owners of the business processes such as the budget pack, the strategy pack, long-term business plans etc., which tend to come out of corporate with all the relevant templates. There is a very strong role for them to be involved and work closely with the risk manager, so that the risk manager can embed the risk management thinking into all those processes ... Where management accountants can I think be useful support is in assisting risk management. The impact aspect sometimes might get quite detailed. You might want to try and come up with a rough number for the impact on the business and clearly they are the guys with some good expertise. But I wouldn't see management accountants driving this, simply because it will become a number crunching exercise and will be viewed as that – whether or not it is – it will still be viewed as that. And management accountants don't have the skill set to drive risk management because it's about cultural change, not about banging out a new process ... the skill set for changing a culture is probably quite different to the skill set for the management accountant. It's a lot more about influencing, changing people's thinking on all those aspects of change management. Now maybe that is part of their skill set, I don't know, but from the people I've met I suspect not.

*Vice President, European federation of risk
management associations*

At one end of the spectrum you have the pure downside risks of the more or less traditional insurance kind of areas. At the other end of the spectrum you have got really what is all around risk and opportunity ... the big decision about going into a new territory, a merger, a new product etc. – the really big ones – they are going to be very risk oriented decisions which will still not be very analysable because that's the very nature of entrepreneurship where you have to have a risk management framework, but it's about decision making ... But there's a whole big raft in the middle between those two extremes, where you can use particular analysis tools, where particularly your management accountants have a key role in looking at different outcomes and different modelling and those type of issues.

*Risk manager, telecommunications
PLC with UK and US listing*

However, respondents did emphasise the distinction between the role of the management accountant and finance director, which had been hinted at in our survey responses.

I've got a financial controller and he looks primarily after the day-to-day number crunching and producing the management reports. I've also got a finance director above him ... he has to understand all the aspects of the business as much as possible and then be able to interpret the financial information and be able to advise on what risks we face ... he acts as a counter balance to my partner and I who are predominantly from a sales background, who are traditionally very optimistic and bullish about the way forward.

Chairman, SME, computer retail

The finance director sits on the risk management committee and he brings his own perspective and we employ a number of management accountants who work alongside the project managers and obviously play a part in their area of expertise, financial risks and so forth. They usually have a view and bring an edge to the thing, which makes sure the financial considerations are being properly taken into account.

Non-executive director, SME, Contracting

The effectiveness of risk management

Some respondents were open about the effectiveness of the processes in place.

Being honest, we don't have a formal risk plan in place at the moment ... We do review risks to the business formally every six months to be consistent with the Turnbull recommendation ... we are obliged to do it in all honesty, but we like to think that it would help us drive our performance and ensure that risks don't overtake any opportunities that the business might have.

Finance Director, subsidiary of listed PLC

But there was a contrasting view.

We have a formal risk management system which I consider to be very effective. We deal with significant contracts and the risks can be significant ... We have an executive risk management committee which reviews proposals for projects and capital investment. We stick to that quite rigorously and it helps us to ensure that risks are being highlighted and managed ... Of course, you have to get people on board or it won't work. Rigid rules can be by-passed and controls can be manipulated – if you have that situation then your risk management is failing.

Non-executive director, SME, Contracting

At the end of the day, the biggest risks to our company is running out of money, so we have extensive management controls in place that tell me exactly where I am with regard to cash … I also have extensive information and feedback with regard to competition, to let me know what's going on in the market … I can't survive without extensive management information … the performance of the sales team … masses of information and statistics, about the utilisation I am getting out of those people … The key is to have the information, study it, but then it is intuition, gut feel, your own interpretation, your own view, in terms of what you do with that information and the timing of when you do it.

Chairman, SME, computer retail

The benefits of risk management

The interviews gave a clear picture of organizations being initially driven by compliance with Turnbull and the Combined Code, but although we only asked survey respondents their perception of risks and benefits, many organisations have realized that tangible business benefits can be achieved.

We asked our interview respondents what the benefits of risk management were, given that around 40 per cent of survey respondents in the FTSE sample did not agree that the benefits of risk management exceeded costs.

That doesn't necessarily surprise me and I think it's a good challenge to say whether we all want to be, as risk management people, in a position where at least 75 per cent think it is of value, well that's where we want to be in two or three or four years time … The way we do that is by really emphasising and creating methodologies which aren't bureaucratic, which are light of touch, which don't stifle, kill, strangle entrepreneurship, but that do add some value.

Risk manager, telecommunications PLC with UK and US listing

I think what risk management is helping to do, is give people more foresight as to what are the risks that may impact me over the next 12 months or 5 years, depending on what your strategy is … you are more likely to have action plans in place, therefore minimising the time you spend fire fighting and hopefully maximising the time you spend developing your objectives.

Group Risk Manager, FTSE company, Financial Services

It's very difficult because what you're dealing with is very subjective ... You do start seeing benefits though, the number of times you get invited to discussions or project control committees and so forth, where your views are actively sought.

Group Risk Manager, FTSE company, Financial Services

Good risk managers are constantly alert to major risks. The Dot Coms did not recognise the risks. Pension funds like Equitable didn't realise the risks they were running, it wasn't on their radar until it was too late ... ABB bought a company with major asbestos liabilities that has almost sunk the company. Risk management is an essential part of due diligence.

Chief Executive, UK association of risk managers

It depends on what you term as the costs and benefits and that is back to the aspect where there is, perhaps, a place for management accountants to actually help bring out some of those numbers. It may be the case that things are not cost effective, but the difficulty is risk management is a long-term investment. It's totally incompatible with short-term business thinking and reporting ... Maybe you have to start amortising some of those risk management costs over a longer period of time ... the major risks might have a one-in-a-hundred years frequency, do you amortise over a hundred years?

Vice President, European federation of risk management associations

Embedding risk management in culture

The third phase of the trend in risk management identified by our survey was risk being used to aid decisions, a significant shift from the 'tick box' approach, where risk management is culturally embedded and taken for granted throughout the organisation. We asked our respondents about this.

The difference between organisations who are excellent at risk management and those who aren't is probably cultural and therefore it kind of flows through as to the type of culture the organisation has. Can you see that from outside? I suspect probably you can to an extent. That's not to say that – I know a lot of people who would then say that if you're bad at risk management you're a bad business – I wouldn't necessarily say that, I don't think that necessarily makes you a bad business. I think it means that you have got to understand the culture of that business and that there are likely to be of a particular type, which will be probably quite a heavy risk taking culture, which will be dominated by an individual or a few individuals or something of that ilk. Now that doesn't make them a bad business ... But the problem with that in the future may come from a mismatch in expectations between what the shareholders of that business actually have and what that business is actually doing. Particularly if you are ticking a whole bunch of boxes that say 'I have good corporate governance' but the reality is that it is a sham.

Risk manager, telecommunications PLC
with UK and US listing

Risk management needs to be embedded in the culture of the company. Some companies have always practised it, for example safety at DuPont. The example of Tylenol at Johnson and Johnson was one of maintaining the integrity of the business.[1] The danger of a strong culture can work against risk, for example at Enron where the culture was to work as close to the line as possible. The problem is stopping the juggernaut and being accused of disloyalty.

Chief Executive, UK association of risk managers

There was a view that much of the cultural embeddedness was a national factor.

I'd have to say that about 90 per cent of what I still see in risk management is still around reducing the negative consequences ... Looking at the upside, it's starting ... it's a gradually evolving process. It's getting that cultural change within the businesses ... The concept of risk management is fairly well accepted in the UK, simply because it's probably been driven by Turnbull and the Combined Code. If you go outside the UK, Germany is fairly well integrated into the thinking, because again they have got corporate governance that reinforces that whole process. The more Latin approach is 'I know how to manage my risks. I'll take the chance' etc., without a logical thinking through, it's a lot more gut instinct. Now some of that works very well and you need to encourage that, otherwise you shut the business down. That's where you get the link between the culture and the processes because, if you haven't got the processes and you haven't got the right culture, the processes either won't be implemented or else they will be implemented in a box-ticking way.

Vice President, European federation of
risk management associations

Perhaps the best example of risk management being embedded in culture came from the international loss prevention manager of a Fortune 500 chemical engineering company.

> If you have a risk management culture then the process of risk management should really be fully integrated with everybody, so you don't need a person strutting around saying 'I am the risk manager' … I'm more comfortable with the term consultant and what I bring to bear in that is experience I have with treatment of risks, which may be insurable or not insurable.

> We have a very strong culture of risk management, as a company we, for about 30 or 35 years, focused very strongly on safety. That's only one risk arena of course, but safety has been held very publicly to be more important than profits, more important than turnover, more important than many other things – more important than anything in fact in our company. And the guy at the top says that every time he starts a major report. As a consequence of that approach we have a world-class safety record and we are certainly the leader, the best, in the chemicals business worldwide.

This comment invited the researchers to question how shareholders perceived safety as more important than profits.

> Inevitably, there are direct savings as a result of not having injuries, there are also indirect savings. Our incident management system looks at everything that happens. It may be a spanner dropping on a workman's head. He may be wearing a hard hat – he should be. There may be a property implication, if that spanner falls into a piece of machinery or arcs some electrical equipment or something like that. Now there's a direct benefit from having fewer injuries … I don't know that it has a direct impact on shareholders, but I think they like the story and frankly, if a company has the best safety record in the business, as a shareholder you would probably like to be associated with that company.

We asked about the evolution from a safety culture to a risk management culture.

> It seems to me that most of the risks that face us are associated with people or the activities of individuals or groups. External risks exist of course, earthquakes and storms, but you can do much more to control behaviour than you can to control the weather or seismic activity … I think that is generally embedding in culture, in people, that you need to have a responsibility for the

safety of colleagues and that you need to do things carefully and check with the right people that you're managing, that you're negotiating the right terms in contracts and that you're running the plant safely.

International loss prevention manager of a Fortune 500 chemical engineering company

Conclusion

We asked a senior risk management professional about the difference between organisations that are seen as very good at risk management and those that are poor at it. His comments provide a powerful conclusion to this chapter.

> From the top level down there will be a different culture within the organisation, where you would have people thinking outside the box in terms of what might knock their plans off course. This would be an organisation that doesn't issue profit warnings, doesn't have major unjustified exceptional costs on its annual accounts because they thought about things in advance. They have managed acquisitions and mergers proactively to ensure that they have met their targets and objectives and haven't impaired the goodwill or asset values. These are some of the things you might see. A profitable and successful company, excellent reputation, corporate social responsibility – you wouldn't see them being fingered as people who are exploiting the third world, child labour, etc. – all those things sort of come out of it. They have got their supply chain issues sorted out. I guess out in the City, analysts are comfortable with what they are hearing and probably their estimates are pretty close to what the organisation achieves. Good credit rating, because they can see that they are good value and their ratios are all good. So all those sort of things ought to be indicators of good risk management. I mean they will also be indicators of other things as well in terms of good general management, performance and risk management is just one aspect of that. That's where you come back to the challenge to identify, you know, the risk management aspects if you are trying to quantify the benefits of risk management because it's sort of mixed in and it ought to be embedded in the thinking, so if it's properly embedded it's almost difficult to bring it out. That's a challenge.

Vice President, European federation of risk management associations

Summary of main interview findings

The traditional approach to risk management was evidenced in many interviews. This revolved around achieving targets, the lack of a structured approach to risk management, an emphasis on being reactive and perceiving the downside of risk rather than risk as missed opportunity.

The drivers of risk management were certainly seen as the increased corporate governance agenda but, equally, so were the increased expectations of investors. This was linked to legitimating activity, part of the 'tick box' compliance approach. There were also examples of business shocks that had resulted in risk management moving up the management agenda. However, interviewees did give examples of the beginning of a shift to a more proactive stance where risk management was seen to deliver business benefits. There was a strong emphasis from our interviewees that this shift was likely to increase with a move away from the 'tick box' approach.

In terms of methods of risk management, our interviewees advised us that 'keeping things simple' was best, although more sophisticated techniques were more likely to be used at lower organizational levels. This was largely because business was so complex and supposedly 'objective' methods may not be reliable. However, many interviewees suggested that there needed to be a balance between the objective information (the role of the accountant) and more subjective methods based on experience and intuition.

Interviewees saw the skill set of management accountants as not being appropriate to a wider involvement in risk management, although their analytic and modelling skills were essential in a supporting role. The distinction between task-oriented management accountants and strategic finance directors was reinforced in our interviews.

The benefits of effective risk management were exemplified by many interviewees, which included both avoiding downside and taking advantage of upside opportunities. However, it was accepted that there was a need culturally to embed risk into organisations as a taken-for-granted practice.

Note

[1]In 1982, the Tylenol scare began when seven individuals died in Chicago after ingesting Extra Strength Tylenol that contained cyanide. While the crime was never solved and Tylenol sales temporarily collapsed, the brand was rebuilt and recovered in only a few years. The scare led to the introduction of tamper-proof packaging for medicines.

Research findings

The literature review

The distinction has been made between event-uncertainty, commonly viewed as risk, and information-uncertainty (Galbraith, 1977). Two of Galbraith's four organisational design strategies – the creation of slack resources, and the creation of self-contained tasks – reduce the need for information processing because of lower performance standards. The other two – investing in vertical information systems, and creating lateral relations – increase the organisational capacity to process information.

We found that risk management systems improved the organisational capacity to process information, through vertical information systems but also through the role of risk managers, whose role was a cross-cutting one. However, accountants were sceptical about the value of the information they produced, which was not shared by non-accountants, who tended to rely on that information.

We noted that risk can be thought about by reference to the existence of internal or external events, information about those events (i.e. their visibility), managerial perception about events and information (i.e. how they are perceived), and how organisations establish tacit/informal or explicit/formal ways of dealing with risk. There is an important distinction between objective, measurable risk and subjective, perceived risk.

Managers do take risks, based on risk preferences at individual and organisational levels (March and Shapira, 1987). Some of these risk preferences vary with national cultures (Hofstede, 1980; Weber and Hsee, 1998), while some are individual traits (Weber and Milliman, 1997).

The 'risk thermostat' (Adams, 1995) recognises that risk propensity varies based on the risk/reward trade-off and how these are balanced against perceptions of danger. At the organisational level, Douglas and Wildavsky (1983) explained risk perception as a cultural process, commenting that each culture, each set of shared values and supporting social institutions is biased toward highlighting certain risks and downplaying others.

We found that this 'socially constructed' view of risk was a better reflection of organisational risk management than rational modelling approaches typified by textbooks and professional training as it reflected the subjectivity of risk perceptions and preferences, cultural constraints and individual traits. The four 'ideal types' developed by Adams (1995) and adapted here as risk stance – risk sceptical (or fatalists), hierarchists, individualists, and risk aware (or egalitarians) – was helpful in our research in understanding individual and organisational risk management practices. The survey found that the risk stance of managers did influence the risk management practices in use.

The regression analysis results suggested that risk stance was a significant moderating influence on methods of risk management and these then led to perceptions of improved performance reported by these firms. It seems that risk management is mostly conceived of as fitting a hierarchist stance in respect of risk management methods, while the risk aware stance was most closely related to supporting policies and culture and risk being factored into plans.

Summary of main case study findings

The conclusions of the four exploratory case studies were:

1. Four domains of risk were observed, reflecting the different social constructions of participants: financial, operational, political and personal.
2. The process and content of budgeting was categorised as risk modelled, risk considered or risk excluded.
3. Risk transfer took place between and within organisations.
4. Managers 'held' risk and provided containment for the anxiety of others.

The four cases illustrate how the different social constructions of participants in the budgeting process influenced the domains – or alternative lenses – through which the process of budgeting took place and how the content of the budget was determined. The *process* of budgeting in all four cases was characterised as risk considered, in which a top-down budgeting process reflected negotiated targets. The *content* of budget documents were risk excluded, being based on a set of single-point estimates, in which all of the significant risks were excluded from the budget itself. The separation of budgeting and risk management had significant consequences for the management of risk as the process of budgeting needs to be considered separately from the content of budget documents.

Summary of main survey findings

The main findings of the survey were:

- ◆ There was little evidence of any contingent explanations for risk management based on either size or business sector. Similarly, respondents' perceptions of the environmental uncertainty and risk facing their organisations were not reported to influence risk management practices in those organisations.
- ◆ CIMA respondents were more risk concerned than the other respondent groups in relation to their organisations, despite having a lower perception of environmental competitive intensity and uncertainty in their industry/sector.
- ◆ Risk management appears to be driven by an institutional response to calls for improved corporate governance which may reflect both protection and economic opportunity. The external drivers of risk management practices, other than competitive intensity, risk or uncertainty, were observed to be external stakeholders and the demands of regulators and legislation, enacted through boards of directors which were likely to exert influence over the policies and methods adopted for risk management.
- ◆ Risk has shifted from being considered tacitly in the past, to being considered more formally in the present and the survey results reflected our respondents' expectation that this trend will shift markedly to a more holistic approach with risk being used to aid decision-making.
- ◆ Risk was seen on an individual level as much about achieving positive consequences as avoiding negative ones. However, organisational risk management was more about avoiding negative consequences.
- ◆ Methods for risk management that were in highest use were the more subjective ones (particularly experience), with quantitative methods used least of all. These results suggested that a heuristic method of risk management is at work in contrast to the systems-based approach that is associated with risk management in much professional training and in the professional literature. It is possible that, even if well developed methods

were in place, managers would always need to transcend them with heuristics.

◆ The reliance on formal accounting-based controls was also called into question by the survey. Importantly, CIMA respondents were less confident in the formal control systems that existed in their organisations, suggesting that the professional knowledge of accountants accommodates an understanding of the limits of accounting information, a knowledge not shared by non-accountants.

◆ There was little integration between management accounting and risk management, and management accountants in the overwhelming majority of organisations were being marginalised in relation to risk management.

◆ Line managers were mostly concerned with identifying risk, analysing and reporting on risk. Finance directors had a major role in analysing and assessing, and reporting and monitoring risk. Deciding on risk management action was predominantly the concern of the chief executive and the board. Management accountants scored lower than internal audit and risk managers on the identification of risk. The finance director was identified with more aspects of risk management than any other role, suggesting that they may have a pivotal role in risk management.

◆ Given the major public visibility of governance requirements, risk management may be seen largely as a compliance exercise. Management action to decrease the likelihood of risk was given the highest ranking, rather than action to achieve organisational objectives.

◆ Traditional methods of managing risk through transfer (insurance, hedging, etc.) were still seen as more effective than more proactive risk management processes.

◆ The results of the regression study showed that risk stance did moderate the perceived usefulness of risk management practices. The main explanatory variables of improved performance were the degree of use of basic methods, the degree of use of technical methods, the degree to which there were supportive policies and cultures and the degree to which risk was factored into plans. This last variable underlined the findings from the exploratory case studies where it was found that risk did not enter the actual budgets but was considered in the processes of budgeting.

◆ The risk aware stance, in attending to both protection and to opportunity, does create organisations to which the capital markets award a lower *beta*, and hence a higher value. The requirements of corporate governance do not necessarily have to work in opposition to economic rationales of risk as opportunity and adventure. This tantalising indication needs some further research.

Summary of main interview findings

The main findings of the interviews carried out to explore the survey findings were:

◆ The traditional approach to risk management revolved around achieving targets, the lack of a structured approach to risk management, an emphasis on being reactive and perceiving the downside of risk rather than risk as missed opportunity.

◆ The drivers of risk management were seen equally to be the enlarged corporate governance agenda and the increased expectations of investors. This was linked to legitimating activity, part of the 'tick box' compliance approach. There were also examples of business shocks that had resulted in risk management moving up the management agenda. There were examples of the beginning of a shift to a more proactive stance where risk management was seen to deliver business benefits. There was a strong emphasis from our interviewees that this shift was likely to increase with a move away from the 'tick box' approach.

◆ In terms of methods of risk management, keeping things simple was seen as the preferred approach, although more sophisticated techniques were more likely to be used at lower organisational levels. This was largely because business was so complex and the supposedly 'objective' methods may not be reliable. However, it was recognised that there needed to be a balance between the objective information (the role of the accountant) and more subjective methods based on experience and intuition.

◆ The skill set of management accountants was not seen as being appropriate to a wider involvement in risk management, although their analytical and modelling skills were essential in a supporting role. There is an important distinction between task-oriented management accountants and strategically-oriented finance directors.

◆ There are important benefits of implementing effective risk management, including both avoiding downside and taking advantage of upside opportunities. However, it was accepted that there was a need culturally to embed risk into organisations as a taken-for-granted practice.

Revised framework for risk management

Figure 3.2 presented a framework for risk management that was tested using the survey results. The survey results show that:

◆ There were no significant correlations to demographic data between either the ownership structure of the organisation or the nature of business, but significant correlations existed between size and the use of risk management methods.

◆ There was an absence of significant correlations between environmental uncertainty and risk and other group variables.

◆ The external drivers of risk management practices were observed to be external stakeholders and the demands of regulators and legislation, enacted through boards of directors.

◆ There was no statistically significant association between risk propensity (risk averse, risk neutral and risk willing) and organisation type, sector, or size.

◆ Organisational risk management was more about avoiding negative consequences, suggesting a protective orientation rather than an opportunistic one.

◆ There are strong and significant relationships between supporting processes and culture and the usage of basic and technical methods of risk management, risks being factored into plans and improved performance and external relationships. However, weaker responses suggested that only about half of respondents' organisations felt that risks were understood and embedded at the cultural level.

◆ A trend in risk management observed here was from risk being considered tacitly in the past to it being considered formally in the present and with the expectation that, in the future, there would be a more holistic approach to risk being used to aid decision-making.

◆ The methods in highest use were the more subjective ones (particularly experience), with quantitative methods used least of all, reinforcing the conjecture that heuristic (or process) mechanisms may be more important for risk management than systematic mechanisms.

◆ There was little integration between management accounting and risk management, and management accountants in the overwhelming majority of organisations were being marginalised in relation to risk management.

◆ Fifty per cent believe the benefits of risk management exceed the costs. However, traditional methods of managing risk through transfer (insurance, hedging, etc.) were still seen as more effective than more proactive risk management processes.

◆ The risk stance (hierarchists, risk aware, entrepreneurs and risk sceptical) did influence the risk management practices in use.

◆ The regression analysis provided some confidence that four variables – basic and technical methods of risk management, supporting processes and culture, and the degree to which risk was factored into budgets and plans – did quite strongly predict reported improvement in performance.

◆ The risk aware stance, in attending to both protection and to opportunity, does create organisations which the capital markets award a lower *beta*, and hence a higher value.

Figure 5.1 reflects the research findings, in particular by reflecting that:

1. There are many external drivers to risk management, not only regulatory but that these are enacted by or through the board of directors.
2. Other than organisation size, there appears to be no correlation between environmental uncertainty or competitive factors and risk management practices.
3. Risk propensity was not as important as risk stance.
4. Risk management practices exist along a continuum of heuristic to systematic but, at corporate level, the heuristic methods dominate.
5. Risk management practices are believed by respondents to move along a life cycle from heuristic to systems dependent to culturally embedded.
6. The involvement of accountants in risk management was marginal.
7. Risk management was perceived to improve organisational performance and there was indication that a risk aware stance could be related to a lower capital market risk profile.

The framework in Figure 5.1, in conjunction with that developed by Solomon et al. (2000) presents a useful model for understanding how risk management practices are introduced and develop over time. The framework does not support the adoption of views expressed in the Turnbull Report (Institute of Chartered Accountants in England & Wales, 1999) and the *Combined Code on Corporate Governance* (Financial Reporting Council, 2003), as risk was still dominated by downside concerns and risk transfer through hedging and insurance remains dominant over proactive risk management. However, the marginalisation of accountants in risk management reinforces the observations made by Spira and Page (2003: p.645).

In this study, at the organisational level, the most significant driver of risk management practice was seen to be corporate governance, enacted through boards of directors and other key stakeholders. This may be seen as constituting a reliance on legitimation, i.e. avoiding the risk of being seen not to have a risk management and

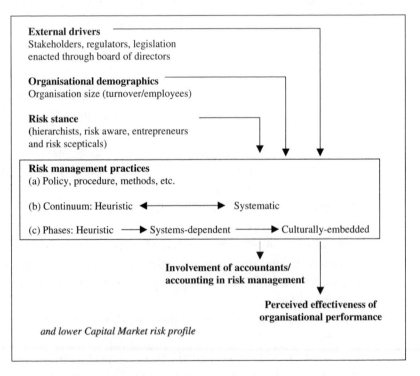

Figure 5.1 Revised framework for risk management practices in organisations

internal control system. While managers reported some influence on risk management practices from markets, the regression analysis demonstrated that this was not definitive. Hence, there was little evidence in the research results that risk management was based upon an analysis of the business in its context, i.e. of the focus of risk management being pushed outwards from the organisation. In the corporate governance approach, risk management was being pushed inwards and downwards to line managers but, given the reported use of 'factoring risks into planning' and in the use of heuristic decision-making, then it may be inferred that corporate governance is not necessarily antithetical to business venturing.

Risk and the social construction of uncertainty

Uncertainty limits the ability of the organisation to make decisions in advance (Galbraith, 1977: p.4). As organisational respondents to this study have not recognised event-uncertainty as anything controllable by risk management, we are left with the notion of risk management applied to task uncertainty. Uncertainty makes a difference to organisation structure and increases the amount of information that must be processed during task execution. Task uncertainty, division of labour, diversity of output and level of performance determine the amount of information that must be processed. Following Galbraith (1974) it can be argued that the greater the risk (task uncertainty) the greater the amount of control is needed in order to achieve a given level of performance. However, the adoption of heuristic techniques suggests that the social constructionist perspective cannot be overlooked by researchers.

Risk management practices existed along a continuum from basic to technical methods, implemented on a continuum from systematic to heuristic. In concert with recent managerial research (e.g. Hellier et al., 2002) but contrary to much of the management science literature, risk management practices reported here emphasise subjective methods rather than sophisticated analytic techniques.

The importance of the social constructions of managers is at the heart of this research which, while applying a positivistic methodology, is based on the social constructions of respondents. The risk stances model developed from the work of Douglas and Wildavsky (1983) and Adams (1995) enables a new understanding of how managers influence risk management and internal control decisions.

The risk sceptical (fatalists in Adams' ideal type) are those who do not see risk management as being important or having any consequences, or were neutral. This group comprised only 7 per cent of the respondents. Entrepreneurs agreed that risk management is about positive consequences but disagreed or were neutral about negative consequences, perhaps a risk seeking group. Hierarchists disagreed or were neutral in relation to positive consequences but agreed in relation to negative ones. This is the risk-avoiding group. The risk aware (Adams' egalitarians) group were balanced between risk management's role in both achieving positive and avoiding negative consequences. This research suggests that this risk aware group would embed risk in culture and decision-making.

This research has provided a snapshot of the social construction of uncertainty involving the bracketing of event-uncertainty, the adoption of a particular stance towards risk and the adoption of risk management and control procedures based on socially constructed risk perceptions and risk propensity, reflected in heuristic approaches to risk management.

The risk of control

There is an implicit assumption in corporate governance literature that the higher the risk (in terms of likelihood and consequence), the higher must be the control of that risk. However, this is a circular argument. Risk is deemed to be high because something is either uncertain or has significant consequences, or both. If the likelihood and consequence of risks could be controlled, then by definition they would not be considered risky. While risk management techniques may be effective for risks over which the organisation has the capacity to exercise control, most external risks are a different matter. Organisations can develop methods of anticipation, contingency plans and adopt flexible practices but, in those cases, 'control' may impede or prevent anticipation, contingency and flexibility. There is then a risk of control (Berry et al., 2005).

Risk management practices may lead to an organisation taking (unwittingly) higher risks. This effect is similar to that discussed by

Adams (1995), where he noted that higher levels of perceived safety might lead individuals with stable risk preferences to undertake more dangerous activities. A first risk of control may have arisen because of the emphasis on controlling threat based upon considerations of compliance to corporate governance imperatives following upon the Turnbull recommendation for a risk-based approach to establishing a system of internal control to provide against worst-case scenarios. This may have carried through into *excessive* control by establishing a range of prescriptive controls such that organisational actions are overly constrained. Organisational participants may have less room to manoeuvre and in a turbulent environment this may result in an increase, rather than a decrease in risk as policies, plans and budgets do not have the flexibility to cope with the unexpected. Further, it may be argued that opportunities may be foreclosed.

A second risk of control is that controls put in place for risk management may have given an unjustifiable confidence that event-uncertainty was being managed. This may have been especially true for those organisations which emphasised both of the aspects of risk management as opportunity or as containing threat.

In this study we were unable to establish the degree to which organisations understood the relationship of the control of risk and the risk of control, even though it was clear that many organisations were reported as having equal attention to threat and opportunity. Nor were we able to examine the differences in the types of control procedures which were designed to deal with the problems of threat and opportunity, except for the possibility that the opportunity risk controls may have been handled in the context of planning and strategic decision-making and that the threat controls may have been handled in the risk management procedures. This was perhaps recognised in the research results that highlighted the organisational preference for the use of heuristic rather than systematic risk management practices.

Limitations of the research

There are a number of limitations to the research study arising from:

◆ The limited number of responses and the non-response bias.
◆ The (deliberate) focus on accountants.

- The corporate level of analysis.
- The design of the survey to collect perceptions of respondents rather than any validated performance data.

Despite these limitations, the survey provides useful insights into enterprise-wide internal control procedures to identify and manage risk and the contribution of, and the consequences for management accountants.

Summary of research and best practice implications

The importance of risk management

CIMA's definition of risk management is the process of under-standing and managing the risks that the organisation is inevitably subject to in attempting to achieve its corporate objectives.

The *Combined Code on Corporate Governance* (Financial Reporting Council, 2003) is established not only as a requirement for listed companies but, increasingly, as a best practice guideline for unlisted companies. However, while corporate governance is an important motivator for risk management and internal control practices (Spira and Page, 2003), it should be remembered that the Turnbull Report emphasised that as profits are, in part, the reward for successful risk taking in business, the purpose of internal control is to help manage and control risk appropriately rather than to eliminate it. The 'illusion of control' (Marshall et al., 1996) or 'risk of control' (Berry et al., 2005) has been suggested, leading to the importance, not just of formal systems of control, but of informal controls, frequently embedded in organisational culture.

Valuable frameworks exist for risk management:

- ◆ The *Risk Management Standard* (Institute of Risk Management, 2002)
- ◆ *Enterprise Risk Management – Integrated Framework* (Committee of Sponsoring Organisations of the Treadway Commission (COSO), 2004)
- ◆ *Enterprise Governance: Getting the Balance Right* (CIMA, 2003).

The changing role of management accountants is also important in establishing the context for their role in risk management and wider views of management control. Risk management is the process by which organisations methodically address the risks attaching to their activities with the goal of achieving sustained benefit within each activity and across the portfolio of all activities. The focus of good risk management is the identification and treatment of these risks consistent with the organisation's risk appetite. Best practice involves making the organisation's risk appetite explicit and com-municating this widely within the organisation.

Enterprise risk management aligns risk management with business strategy and embeds a risk management culture into business oper-ations. It encompasses the whole organisation and sees risks as

113

opportunities to be grasped as much as hazards. It is generally agreed among professional risk managers that the future management of risk will be fostering a change in the risk culture of the organisation towards one where risks are considered as a normal part of the management process. Best practice involves establishing an appropriate risk management system, but recognising that the system may achieve little without a culture that supports the organisational approach to managing risk.

We have very little understanding of how managers in organisations perceive and take risks or of the commonalities or differences between individual risk taking and risk taking by managers in the organisational context.

Managers perceive risk differently and assess the risk/return trade-off in different ways. Everyone has a propensity to take risks but the propensity varies from person to person. The propensity to take risks is influenced by the potential rewards of risk taking and experience of 'accidents' that cause losses. Individual risk taking therefore is a balance between perceptions of risk and the propensity to take risks.

Research has found that attitudes towards risk taking or risk avoidance exist as a trait on a continuum from risk avoiding to risk taking. Risk perception is also a cultural process, sometimes at a national level and sometimes at an organisational level, even at an occupational level (e.g. accountants are often stereotyped as being risk averse). Each culture, each set of shared values and supporting social institutions is biased toward highlighting certain risks and downplaying others. Research has also found that managers rely on instinct and experience in forming judgements about risk. Best practice involves understanding how managers perceive risks, and their attitude to risk taking, given the organisational culture and its appetite for risk.

Boards of directors have a responsibility under the Combined Code to maintain a sound system of internal control to safeguard shareholders' investment and the company's assets. Best practice involves adopting a risk-based approach to internal control and a continual review of its effectiveness. The purpose of internal control is to help manage and control risk appropriately rather than to eliminate it.

The COSO *Enterprise Risk Management Framework* is considered a model of best practice. Its approach to risk-based internal control contains eight components – internal environment, objective setting, event identification, risk assessment, risk response, control activities, information and communication, and monitoring.

There has been an implicit assumption in much research that management control systems play an important part in risk management. However, an excess of controls can produce an 'illusion of control'. One risk of control is that the existence of controls may lead managers to believe that risks are well controlled, and unforeseen circumstances may arise or opportunities may be missed because of an over-reliance on controls. A second risk of control is that the existence of controls prevents any risky activities from being undertaken which leads to missed opportunities. Best practice involves recognising that, while risk-based controls are essential to manage risks, excessive controls, or an over-reliance on formal controls, can be counter-productive.

Management accountants are involved in internal control mechanisms, whether the controls are financial or non-financial. These controls include planning, information for decision-making, traditional financial controls, such as budgeting and management reporting, and balanced scorecard-type systems of non-financial performance measurement. However, the decentring of accounting knowledge in many organisations and the increase in technology, which has eliminated many routine accounting tasks, means that best practice for management accountants is to move beyond their traditional role and emphasise adding value to their organisations. In the context of this report, this means taking a wider perspective on strategy, risk and management controls, beyond the traditional focus on what is measurable. A 2002 report produced by CIMA argued that management accountants, whose professional training includes the analysis of information and systems, performance and strategic management, can have a significant role to play in developing and implementing risk management and internal control systems within their organisations.

This wider view was evidenced in the four case studies described in the report. The four cases illustrate how the different social constructions of participants in the budgeting process influenced the domains – or alternative lenses – through which the process of budgeting took place and how the content of the budget was determined. Different 'domains of risk' reflected the different social constructions of participants.

There was little direct evidence of 'risk modelling' in the four cases and a minor reflection of risk consideration in one case. The *process* of budgeting in all four cases was characterised as 'risk considered', in which a top-down budgeting process reflected negotiated targets. The *content* of budget documents were 'risk excluded', being based on a set of single-point estimates, in which all of the significant risks were excluded from the budget itself. In terms of best practice, the separation of budgeting and risk management has significant consequences for the management of risk as the case studies suggested that there is a relationship between the social constructions of budget participants at different levels of analysis that impacts the budgeting process. In particular, the process of budgeting, by excluding some risks and considering others, is seen to be different to, and needs to be interpreted separately, from the content of the budget.

While we did not identify best practice in these cases, we considered that best practice involved moving beyond a narrow focus of accounting or broader quantitative issues and addressing the social constructions of participants in the budget process. We thought that these findings may be generalisable beyond budgets to other forms of management control. Given that the case studies suggested that the most significant risks may be excluded from financial reports, the requirements of governance and internal control motivated us to consider in greater depth the relationship between risk and management control, and the role of management accountants in that dynamic.

Research conclusions

The main conclusions from the research were that:

◆ The framework of risk management practice describes the antecedents of risk management practice and reflects both a continuum from heuristic to systematic policies, procedures and methods.

- Heuristic methods of risk management were used much more than the systems-based approach that is associated with risk management in much of the literature, at least at the corporate level of risk management. The methods in highest use were the more subjective ones (particularly experience), with quantitative methods used least of all. It is suspected that crucial assessments of risk were undertaken in managerial dialogues rather than in any final risk management process, reinforcing the role of the human actor over analytical techniques. There was also evidence of significant reliance on external advisers.
- The organisational stance towards risk (risk sceptical, hierarchists, entrepreneurs and risk aware) was an important determinant of risk management practices.
- The 'trend' model demonstrates the perception by respondents of a shift over time from risk being considered tacitly in the past to it being considered more formally at the present, with the expectation of respondents that, in the future, there will be a more holistic approach with risk being culturally embedded and used to aid decision-making.
- Risk management practices in use were perceived by respondents to have delivered benefits that exceed the cost.
- CIMA respondents were more sceptical about the value of accounting-based tools and controls than other respondents.
- The finance director was identified with more aspects of risk management than any other role, suggesting that they may have a pivotal role in risk management. However, management accountants in the majority of organisations were being marginalised in relation to risk management. CIMA respondents indicated that management accountants should have more involvement in risk management, although this was not a view shared by other respondents.

The results suggested that risk management practice was driven institutionally rather than strategically or economically. The response by organisations has not been to the logic of markets in terms of competitive intensity and environmental uncertainty but more an institutional response to calls for improved corporate governance. Risk management may therefore be more about protection against the uncertainties of the internal world, however that may be perceived, rather than about protection against or engaging with uncertainties of the external world.

Summary of research findings and implications for best practice

Main survey findings and best practice implications

Contrary to expectations that risk management practices vary between organisations as a result of their size or industry sector, there was little evidence of any contingent explanations for risk management based on either size or business sector. Similarly, respondents' perceptions of the environmental uncertainty and risk facing their organisations did not appear to influence risk management practices in those organisations.

However, perhaps reinforcing traditional stereotypes, CIMA respondents were more risk concerned than the other respondent groups in relation to their organisations, despite having a lower perception of the competitive intensity and uncertainty in their industry/sector.

These survey results suggested that risk management was driven by an institutional response to calls for improved corporate governance which may reflect both protection and economic opportunity. The external drivers of risk management practices, other than competitive intensity, risk or uncertainty, were observed to be external stakeholders and the demands of regulators and legislation, enacted through boards of directors which were likely to exert influence over the policies and methods adopted for risk management.

However, risk has shifted from being considered tacitly to being considered more formally and the survey results reflected our respondents' expectation that this trend will shift markedly to a more holistic approach with risk being used to aid decision-making. Although our research found that adherence to the regulatory environment is essential, we would suggest that *best practice goes much further than this, emphasising the importance of culturally-embedding risk awareness in organisations.*

Risk was seen on an individual level as much about achieving positive consequences as avoiding negative ones. However, organisational risk management was more about avoiding negative consequences. *Best practice is likely to emphasise a broader opportunistic approach to risk management, based on a risk/return trade-off, rather than a purely defensive or protective stance.*

The survey found that the methods for risk management that were in highest use were the more subjective ones (particularly experience), with quantitative methods used least of all. There was also significant reliance on external advisers. These results suggested a heuristic method of risk management is at work in contrast to the systems-based approach that is associated with risk management in much professional training and in the professional literature. As previously stated, *best practice will involve using appropriate and effective tools, but these tools should be supplemented by experience, intuition and judgement.*

The reliance on formal accounting-based controls was also called into question. Importantly, CIMA respondents were less confident in the formal control systems that existed in their organisations, suggesting that the professional knowledge of accountants accommodates an understanding of the limits of accounting information, a knowledge not shared by non-accountants. *Best practice may therefore involve the training of users of financial information in the limitations of that information.*

The responses reveal that line managers were mostly concerned with identifying risk, analysing and reporting on risk. Finance directors had a major role in analysing and assessing, and reporting and monitoring risk. Deciding on risk management action was predominantly the concern of the chief executive and the board. Management accountants scored lower than internal audit and risk managers on the identification of risk. The finance director was identified with more aspects of risk management than any other role, suggesting that they may have a pivotal role in risk management. The distinction here between the role of the management accountant and finance director is an important one. *The best practice implication for CIMA is that their members may have to reach finance director positions before they can contribute more significantly to risk management, but clearly they should be educated to be able to fulfil that function.*

There was little integration between management accounting and risk management, and management accountants in the overwhelming majority of organisations were being marginalised in relation to risk management. While CIMA respondents feel that management accountants should have more involvement in risk management, this was not a view shared by other respondents. *Best practice, at least for management accountants, appears to be a shift towards a more strategic and value adding role which, by definition, includes a consideration of risk.* This is consistent with the literature on the changing role of the accountant.

Given the major publicity and governance requirements, risk management may be seen largely as a compliance exercise. However, half of the respondents reported that the benefits exceeded the costs. Perhaps unsurprisingly, management action to decrease the likelihood of risk was given the highest ranking, rather than action to achieve organisational objectives. The survey responses implied that traditional methods of managing risk through transfer (insurance, hedging, etc.) were still seen as more effective than more proactive risk management processes. *Best practice involves a deliberately proactive stance towards risk management, rather than an excessive reliance on traditional techniques, except to the extent that these techniques remain useful.*

In relation to financial market risk, the implication of our regression analysis is that the risk aware stance, in attending to both protection and to opportunity, did create organisations to which the capital markets award a lower average *beta* and, hence, a higher value. It is interesting too that it is both the stance and the factoring of risk into plans that is related. This led us to infer that the requirements of corporate governance do not necessarily have to work in opposition to economic rationales of risk as opportunity and adventure. However, given the small samples, this observation is indicative only and would need to be replicated on a larger scale.

Results of interviews to explore survey findings and best practice implications

The traditional approach to risk management was evidenced in many interviews. This revolved around achieving targets, the lack of a structured approach to risk management, an emphasis on being reactive and perceiving the downside of risk rather than risk as missed opportunity.

The drivers of risk management were certainly seen as the increased corporate governance agenda but, equally, the increased expectations of investors. This was linked to legitimating activity, part of the 'tick box' compliance approach. There were also examples of business shocks that had resulted in risk management moving up the management agenda. However, interviewees did give examples of the beginning of a shift to a more proactive stance where risk management was seen to deliver business benefits. There was a strong emphasis from our interviewees that this shift was likely to increase with a move away from the 'tick box' approach.

In terms of methods of risk management, our interviewees advised that keeping things simple was best, although more sophisticated techniques were more likely to be used at lower organisational levels. This was largely because business was so complex and supposedly 'objective' methods may not be reliable. However, many interviewees suggested that there needed to be a balance between the objective information (the role of the accountant) and more subjective methods based on experience and intuition.

Interviewees saw the skill set of management accountants as not being appropriate to a wider involvement in risk management, although their analytic and modelling skills were essential in a supporting role. The distinction between task-oriented management accountants and strategic finance directors was reinforced in our interviews.

The benefits of effective risk management were exemplified by many interviewees, which included both avoiding downside and taking advantage of upside opportunities. However, it was accepted that there was a need culturally to embed risk into organisations as a taken-for-granted practice.

Summary of best practice implications

Institutional investors are likely to value more highly a well-governed company. Being well governed includes having an effective risk management system with a risk aware stance.

In the UK, standards of corporate governance are established in the *Combined Code on Corporate Governance*, which adopts a 'comply or explain' approach. In the USA, Sarbanes-Oxley is dominant, with criminal penalties for misleading investors through financial statements. In South Africa, the stakeholder approach adopted by the

King Report takes a wider view of governance. Best practice implies adopting both the spirit and letter of corporate governance regulation. In the UK, the Combined Code requires that boards of directors identify, evaluate and manage significant risks in their organisations.

The traditional accounting and finance approach to risk uses techniques such as decision trees, probability distributions, cost-volume-profit analysis, discounted cash flows, investment portfolios, capital assets pricing model, and hedging techniques to reduce currency and interest rate exposure. Research has identified the role of budgets in relation to risk. By excluding some risks and considering others, the process of constructing a budget was seen to be different to and interpreted separately from the content of the budget (document) in which there was little evidence of risk modelling or the use of probabilities.

The value of quantification as a technique for managing risk is not universally accepted. This is because many risks are not objectively identifiable and measurable but subjective and qualitative. For example, the risks of litigation, economic downturns, loss of key employees, natural disasters, and loss of reputation are all subjective judgements. Risk is, therefore, to a considerable extent, 'socially constructed' and responses to risk need to reflect the perceptions and social constructions of organisational participants.

Using a broader perspective like this, risk can be thought about by reference to:

♦ the existence of internal or external events
♦ information about those events (i.e. their visibility)
♦ managerial perception about events and information (i.e. how they are perceived) and
♦ how organisations establish tacit/informal or explicit/formal ways of dealing with risk.

Best practice involves recognizing that information about risks may be partial and unreliable and that risks are perceived in different ways. It is important to use the available quantitative tools and techniques where it is appropriate to do so, but to recognize that subjective judgements need to be made as part of considering risk.

Shareholders understand the risk/return trade-off as they invest in companies and expect boards to achieve a higher return than is possible from risk-free investments, such as government securities. This implies that they expect boards and managers to be entrepreneurial, but that risks taken will be considered and managed within the accepted risk profile of the organisation.

The focus of risk has shifted from a negative concept of hazard and loss to a positive interpretation that managing risk is an integral part of generating sustainable shareholder value. Risk is therefore best understood as uncertain future events which could influence the achievement of the organisation's strategic, operational and financial objectives. The Institute of Risk Management has defined risk as the combination of the probability of an event and its consequences, with risk management being concerned with both positive and negative aspects of risk. Best practice involves recognising the risk/return trade-off and both the upside (opportunities) and downside (loss) elements of risk.

Implications for risk managers and management accountants

There are a number of implications of the study that are applicable to both risk managers and management accountants:

◆ The imbalance between risk as opportunity and risk as hazard needs to be addressed.
◆ While analytic methods are important and, where used, are effective, the human actor is of most importance, in terms of experience, intuition, hindsight and judgement.
◆ Risk management practices are being developed, but there is still some way to go before these are embedded in management practices. The Phases model in Figure 3.3 may identify the desire (but not the difficulty) of linking risk management practices with organisational decision-making.
◆ Risk management may lead to the 'risk of control': an over-confidence in the ability to manage threats while not adequately addressing risk associated with opportunities.
◆ Although management accountants are more risk averse than other respondents, this may be what organisations want their accountants to be. However, to develop from management accountants to finance directors requires a broader understanding of the identification, assessment and management of risk.

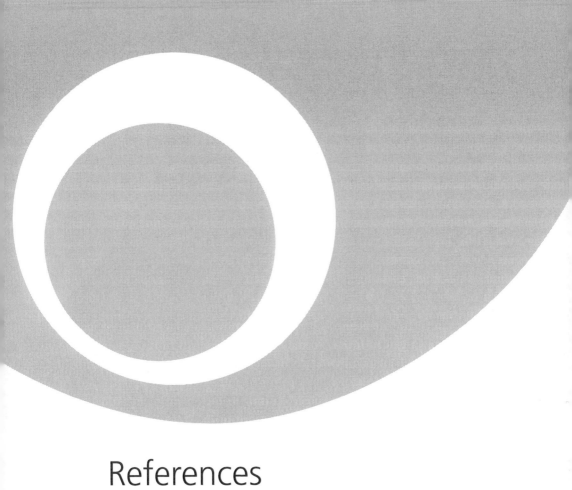

References

Adams J (1995) *Risk*. London: UCL Press

Beck U (1986, 1992 in translation) *Risk Society*. London: Sage

Berry AJ, Broadbent J, Otley D (1995) Procedures for control. In *Management Control: Theories, Issues and Practices*, (AJ Berry, J Broadbent, D Otley, eds). London: Macmillan

Berry AJ, Collier PM, Helliar CV (2005) Risk and control: the control of risk and the risk of control. In *Management Control: Theories, Issues and Performance*, 2nd edn, (AJ Berry, J Broadbent, D Otley, eds). Basingstoke: Palgrave Macmillan, pp. 279–99

Bettis RA, Thomas H (1990) *Risk, Strategy, and Management*. Greenwich, Conn: JAI Press

Bhattachayra S, Behara SA, Gunderson DE (2003) Business risk perspectives on information systems outsourcing. *International Journal of Accounting Information Systems*, 4:75–93

Bussen W, Myers MD (1997) Executive information system failure: a New Zealand case study. *Journal of Information Technology*, 12:145–153

Cadbury Code (1992) *Report of the Committee on the Financial Aspects of Corporate Governance: The Code of Best Practice*. London: Professional Publishing

Chartered Institute of Management Accountants (1999) *Corporate Governance: History, Practice and Future*. London: CIMA Publishing

Chartered Institute of Management Accountants (2002) *Risk Management: A Guide to Good Practice*. London: CIMA Publishing

Chartered Institute of Management Accountants (2003) *Enterprise Governance: Getting the Balance Right*. London: CIMA/IFAC

Chartered Institute of Management Accountants (2005) *CIMA Official Terminology: 2005 edition*. Oxford: Elsevier

Collier PM, Agyei-Ampomah S (2005) *Management Accounting – Risk and Control Strategy*. Oxford: Elsevier

Collier PM, Berry AJ (2002) Risk in the process of budgeting. *Management Accounting Research*, 13:273–297

Committee of Sponsoring Organisations of the Treadway Commission (COSO) (1992) *Internal Control – Integrated Framework*

Committee of Sponsoring Organisations of the Treadway Commission (COSO) (2003) *Enterprise Risk Management Framework*

Committee of Sponsoring Organisations of the Treadway Commission (COSO) (2004) *Enterprise Risk Management – Integrated Framework*

Committee on Corporate Governance (1998) *Final Report* (Hampel Committee). http://www.ecgi.org/codes/documents/hampel.pdf

Davies D (2002a) Risk management – protecting reputation. *Computer Law and Security Report*, 18:414–420

Davies D (2002b) World Trade Centre Lessons. *Computer Law and Security Report*, 18:117–119

Douglas M, Wildavsky A (1983) *Risk and Culture: An Essay on the Selection of Technological and Environmental Dangers.* Los Angeles: University of California Press

Financial Reporting Council (2003) *The Combined Code on Corporate Governance*

Galbraith J (1977) *Designing Complex Organizations.* Reading, Mass.: Addison-Wesley Publishing Company

Galbraith JR (1974) Organizational design: an information processing view. *Interfaces*, 4:28–36

Greenbury, R. (1995) *Directors' Remuneration: Report of a Study Group Chaired by Sir Richard Greenbury.* http://www.ecgi.org/codes/documents/greenbury.pdf

Harris EP (1999) Project risk assessment: a European field study. *British Accounting Review*, 31:347–371

Harris EP (2000) Strategic investment decision-making: managerial judgement on project risk and return. *Journal of Applied Accounting Research*, 5:87–110

Helliar CV, Lonie AA, Power DM, Sinclair CD (2001) *Managerial Attitudes to Risk.* Edinburgh: Institute of Chartered Accountants of Scotland

Helliar CV, Lonie AA, Power DM, Sinclair CD (2002) Managerial attitudes to risk: a comparison of Scottish chartered accountants and UK managers. *Journal of International Accounting, Auditing & Taxation*, 11:156–190

Higgs, D. (2003) *Review of the Role and Effectiveness of Non-executive Directors*. Department of Trade and Industry http://www.dti.gov.uk/files/file23012.pdf?pubpdfdload=03%2F636

Hofstede G (1980) *Culture's Consequences: International Differences in Work Related Values*. Beverly Hills: Sage Publications

Institute of Chartered Accountants in England & Wales (1999) *Internal Control: Guidance for Directors on the Combined Code*, (Turnbull Report)

Institute of Risk Management (2002) *A Risk Management Standard*. London: IRM

International Federation of Accountants (1999) *Enhancing Shareholder Wealth by Better Managing Business Risk. Rep. International Management Accounting Study No. 9*

Jiang JJ, Klein G (1999) Risks to different aspects of systems success. *Information and Management*, 36:263–272

Knight, F.H. (1921). *Risk, Uncertainty, and Profit*. Boston MA, Houghton Mifflin Co.

KPMG (2003) Programme Management Survey 2002–3. http://www.kpmg.com.au/Portals/0/irmprm_pm-survey2003.pdf

Kumar RL (2002) Managing risks in IT projects; an options perspective. *Information and Management*, 40:63–74

Liebenberg AP, Hoyt RE (2003) The determinants of enterprise risk management: evidence from appointment of chief risk officers. *Risk Management and Insurance Review*, 6:1

March JG, Shapira Z (1987) Managerial perspectives on risk and risk taking. *Management Science*, 33:1404–1418

Marshall C, Prusak L, Shpilberg D (1996) Financial risk and the need for superior knowledge management. *California Management Review* 38:77–101

McGoun EG (1995) The history of risk 'measurement'. *Critical Perspectives on Accounting*, 6:511–532

McKinsey & Co (2006) *McKinsey on Finance*. No. 18 http://corporatefinance.mckinsey.com/_downloads/knowledge/mckinsey_on_finance/MoF_Issue_18.pdf

Miller R, Lessard D (2001) Understanding and managing risks in large engineering projects. *International Journal of Project Management*, 19:437–443

Parker LD (2001) Back to the future: the broadening accounting trajectory. *British Accounting Review*, 33: 421–453

Scapens RW, Ezzamel M, Burns J, Baldvinsdottir G (2003) *The Future Direction of UK Management Accounting Practice*. Oxford: Elsevier

Shrivastava P (1993) The greening of business. In *Business and the Environment: Implications of the new Environmentalism*, (D Smith, ed.). London: Paul Chapman Publishing

Smith, R. (2003) *Audit Committees: Combined Code Guidance*. Financial Reporting Council http://www.frc.org.uk/images/uploaded/documents/ACReport.pdf

Solomon JF, Solomon A, Norton SD (2000) A conceptual framework for corporate risk disclosure emerging from the agenda for corporate governance reform. *British Accounting Review*, 32: 447–478

Spira LF, Page M (2003) Risk management: The reinvention of internal control and the changing role of internal audit. *Accounting, Auditing & Accountability Journal*, 16:640–661

Treadway Commission (1987) *Report of the National Commission on Fraudulent Financial Reporting*. http://www.coso.org/NCFFR.pdf

Weber EU, Hsee C (1998) Cross-cultural differences in risk perception, but cross-cultural similarities in attitudes towards perceived risk. *Management Science*, 44:1205–1217

Weber EU, Milliman RA (1997) Perceived risk attitudes: relating risk perception to risky choice. *Management Science*, 43:123–144

Appendix 1

CIMA

Risk Management Questionnaire
The information in your reply will be retained in strict confidence

ASTON
BUSINESS SCHOOL

Section 1. About you

Years worked in current role:

	< 2 years	2-5 years	5-10 years	10-15 years	>15 years
1.1 Current job title: --	☐	☐	☐	☐	☐

	Refuse to take risks	Prefer not to take risks	Neutral	Willing to take risks	Keen to take risks
1.2 How would you describe your <u>personal</u> propensity to take risks:	☐	☐	☐	☐	☐

	Reduced significantly	Reduced a little	Not changed	Increased a little	Increased significantly
1.3 Over the last two years, has your <u>personal</u> propensity to take risks:	☐	☐	☐	☐	☐

1.4 To what extent do you <u>personally</u> agree/disagree with the following statements about risk management:

	Strongly disagree	Disagree	Neutral	Agree	Strongly agree
i. Risk management is about avoiding negative consequences	☐	☐	☐	☐	☐
ii. Risk management is about achieving positive consequences	☐	☐	☐	☐	☐
iii. Risk management should be more a matter of personal judgement	☐	☐	☐	☐	☐
iv. Risk management should be handled through a formal control system that identifies, manages and reports risk	☐	☐	☐	☐	☐

	None	1-19%	20-39%	40-59%	60-79%	80-100%
1.5 What proportion of your work time is spent dealing with risk management:	☐	☐	☐	☐	☐	☐

1.6 Do you <u>personally</u> feel that your level of involvement in risk management is:

	(a)	Insufficient	About right	Too involved	No view
		☐	☐	☐	☐
	(b)	Increasing	Not changing	Decreasing	No view
		☐	☐	☐	☐

Section 2. Your organisation

2.0. Is your organisation part of a group of companies: No ☐ (Go to 2.2)   Yes ☐ (Go to 2.1)

2.1 Please indicate where your organisation sits within the group: Parent ☐   Subsidiary ☐

2.2. What is the ownership structure of your organisation:
- Listed PLC ☐
- Unlisted PLC ☐
- Limited company ☐
- Not-for-profit ☐
- Public sector ☐

2.3. Which best describes the nature of your business:
- Manufacturer/construction ☐
- Retail/distribution ☐
- Finance/insurance ☐
- Services ☐
- Other ☐

2.4. Approximate company turnover (£m):
- < £3m ☐
- £3m - £11m ☐
- £11 - £50m ☐
- £50m - £100m ☐
- £100m - £500m ☐
- > £500m ☐

2.5. Approximate number of employees:
- < 250 ☐
- 250 - 1 000 ☐
- 1 001 - 3 000 ☐
- 3 001 - 5 000 ☐
- 5 001 - 10 000 ☐
- > 10 000 ☐

2.6 What is the degree of:

	Very low	Low	Medium	High	Very high
i. Competitive intensity in your industry/sector	☐	☐	☐	☐	☐
ii. Uncertainty in your industry/sector environment	☐	☐	☐	☐	☐
iii. Risk faced by your organisation	☐	☐	☐	☐	☐
iv. Risk faced within your industry/sector	☐	☐	☐	☐	☐

Appendix 1

133

2.7 To what extent is:

	Decreasing rapidly	Decreasing slowly	Not changing	Increasing slowly	Increasing rapidly
i. Competitive intensity in your industry/sector	☐	☐	☐	☐	☐
ii. Uncertainty in your industry/sector environment	☐	☐	☐	☐	☐
iii. Risk faced by your organisation	☐	☐	☐	☐	☐
iv. Risk faced within your industry/sector	☐	☐	☐	☐	☐

2.8 To what extent do you agree/disagree that the following are drivers of risk management in your organisation:

	Strongly disagree	Disagree	Neutral	Agree	Strongly agree
i. Legislation (including Combined Code and Turnbull Report)	☐	☐	☐	☐	☐
ii. Regulatory bodies	☐	☐	☐	☐	☐
iii. Expectations of shareholders/analysts	☐	☐	☐	☐	☐
iv. The competitive business environment	☐	☐	☐	☐	☐
v. Customers/clients who demand it	☐	☐	☐	☐	☐
vi. A critical event or near miss	☐	☐	☐	☐	☐
vii. Board/top management	☐	☐	☐	☐	☐

viii. Are there other drivers of risk management in your organisation? **Yes** ☐ (Please describe below) **No** ☐

2.9 To what extent do you agree/disagree with the following statements:

	Strongly disagree	Disagree	Neutral	Agree	Strongly agree
i. Your organisation has an effective risk management policy	☐	☐	☐	☐	☐
ii. Risks are well understood throughout your organisation	☐	☐	☐	☐	☐
iii. Controlling risk is highly centralised within your organisation	☐	☐	☐	☐	☐
iv. Your organisation regularly reviews internal controls	☐	☐	☐	☐	☐
v. Risk management is embedded in your organisation's culture	☐	☐	☐	☐	☐
vi. Formal procedures are in place for reporting risks	☐	☐	☐	☐	☐
vii. The level of internal control is appropriate for the risks faced	☐	☐	☐	☐	☐
viii. Your organisation is effective at prioritising risks	☐	☐	☐	☐	☐
ix. Changes to risks are assessed and reported on an ongoing basis	☐	☐	☐	☐	☐

2.10 How would you describe your <u>organisation's</u> propensity to take risks:

Refuse to take risks	Prefer not to take risks	Neutral	Willing to take risks	Keen to take risks
☐	☐	☐	☐	☐

2.11 Over the last two years, has your organisation's propensity to take risks:

Reduced significantly	Reduced a little	Not changed	Increased a little	Increased significantly
☐	☐	☐	☐	☐

2.12 To what extent do you agree/disagree that risk management in your organisation is:

	Strongly disagree	Disagree	Neutral	Agree	Strongly agree
i. About avoiding negative consequences	☐	☐	☐	☐	☐
ii. About achieving positive consequences	☐	☐	☐	☐	☐
iii. More a matter of personal judgement	☐	☐	☐	☐	☐
iv. Handled through a formal control system that identifies, manages and reports risk	☐	☐	☐	☐	☐

2.13 Of the four approaches set out below, which <u>ONE statement</u> best describes your organisations: i) historical, ii) current and iii) planned approach to risk management:

	i Historical approach 2 years ago ✓ One	ii Current approach ✓ One	iii Planned approach next 2 years ✓ One
• Risk is not considered	☐	☐	☐
• Risk is considered tacitly, but not documented or formally managed	☐	☐	☐
• Risk is considered and formally documented in a systematic way	☐	☐	☐
• Risk is considered, documented and used to aid decision-making throughout the business	☐	☐	☐

2.14 Who in your organisation is primarily accountable for:

	(a) Identifying risks	(b) Analysing & assessing risks	(c) Deciding on risk management action	(d) Reporting & monitoring risk
i. CEO/managing director	☐	☐	☐	☐
ii. The board/audit committee	☐	☐	☐	☐
iii. Director of finance	☐	☐	☐	☐
iv. Internal audit	☐	☐	☐	☐
v. Risk manager or similar post	☐	☐	☐	☐
vi. Management accountant	☐	☐	☐	☐
vii. Line managers	☐	☐	☐	☐
viii. Other (please specify below)	☐	☐	☐	☐

2.15 To what extent do you agree/disagree that the following are involved in your organisation's risk management:

	Strongly disagree	Disagree	Neutral	Agree	Strongly agree
i. Shareholders/analysts	☐	☐	☐	☐	☐
ii. Suppliers	☐	☐	☐	☐	☐
iii. Customers	☐	☐	☐	☐	☐
iv. Banks/financiers	☐	☐	☐	☐	☐

2.16 To what extent do you agree/disagree that your organisation's management accounting and risk management functions are integrated:

Strongly disagree	Disagree	Neutral	Agree	Strongly agree
☐	☐	☐	☐	☐

2.17 In terms of risk management, do you feel that the level of involvement of management accounting in your organisation is:

(a)	Insufficient	About right	Too involved	No view
	☐	☐	☐	☐

(b)	Increasing	Not changing	Decreasing	No view
	☐	☐	☐	☐

2.18 To what extent are the following methods:

	(a) Used by your organisation to manage risk:					(b) Effective in helping your organisation to manage risk:				
	Low		Med		High	Low		Med		High
	1	2	3	4	5	1	2	3	4	5
i. Experience, intuition, hindsight, judgement	☐	☐	☐	☐	☐	☐	☐	☐	☐	☐
ii. Brainstorming, scenario analysis, PEST or SWOT analysis	☐	☐	☐	☐	☐	☐	☐	☐	☐	☐
iii. Interviews, surveys, questionnaires	☐	☐	☐	☐	☐	☐	☐	☐	☐	☐
iv. Likelihood/consequences matrix	☐	☐	☐	☐	☐	☐	☐	☐	☐	☐
v. Use of auditors or external consultants	☐	☐	☐	☐	☐	☐	☐	☐	☐	☐
vi. Stochastic modelling, statistical analysis	☐	☐	☐	☐	☐	☐	☐	☐	☐	☐
vii. Risk management software	☐	☐	☐	☐	☐	☐	☐	☐	☐	☐
viii. Monitoring risks using a risk register or written reports	☐	☐	☐	☐	☐	☐	☐	☐	☐	☐
ix. Other (please specify below)	☐	☐	☐	☐	☐	☐	☐	☐	☐	☐

2.19 When formulating the following plans:

	(a) Where is risk considered in the process:				(b) To what extent are risks identified and factored in:				
	Not considered	At the start	Throughout	Subsequent review	Not at all				Fully
					1	2	3	4	5
i. Strategic plans	☐	☐	☐	☐	☐	☐	☐	☐	☐
ii. Budgets	☐	☐	☐	☐	☐	☐	☐	☐	☐
iii. Operational plans	☐	☐	☐	☐	☐	☐	☐	☐	☐
iv. Project management	☐	☐	☐	☐	☐	☐	☐	☐	☐
v. One-off events (e.g. mergers)	☐	☐	☐	☐	☐	☐	☐	☐	☐
vi. Capital investment	☐	☐	☐	☐	☐	☐	☐	☐	☐

2.20 To what extent are the following risk management options:

(a) Used by your organisation to manage risk:

	Low		Med		High
	1	2	3	4	5

(b) Effective in helping your organisation to manage risks

	Low		Med		High
	1	2	3	4	5

i. Transferring the risk using insurance, hedging, contracts, joint ventures or partnerships, etc. ☐ ☐ ☐ ☐ ☐   ☐ ☐ ☐ ☐ ☐

ii. Decreasing the likelihood of the risk through management action, e.g. quality management, project management, R&D, training, etc. ☐ ☐ ☐ ☐ ☐   ☐ ☐ ☐ ☐ ☐

iii. Decreasing adverse consequences of the risk using contingency, business continuity, fraud control plans, etc. ☐ ☐ ☐ ☐ ☐   ☐ ☐ ☐ ☐ ☐

2.21 To what degree has risk management improved performance and or outcomes in your organisation's:

	No improvement	Some improvement		Significant improvement
	1	2	3	4	5

i. Corporate planning ☐ ☐ ☐ ☐ ☐

ii. Resource allocation and utilisation ☐ ☐ ☐ ☐ ☐

iii. Management reporting ☐ ☐ ☐ ☐ ☐

iv. Communication within the organisation ☐ ☐ ☐ ☐ ☐

v. Relationships with shareholders ☐ ☐ ☐ ☐ ☐

vi. Relationships with customers/clients ☐ ☐ ☐ ☐ ☐

vii. Relationships with suppliers ☐ ☐ ☐ ☐ ☐

viii. Management of organisational change ☐ ☐ ☐ ☐ ☐

ix. Reputation ☐ ☐ ☐ ☐ ☐

x. Recognition and uptake of opportunities ☐ ☐ ☐ ☐ ☐

xi. Employee confidence in carrying out their duties ☐ ☐ ☐ ☐ ☐

xii. Are there any other improvements or benefits that have been realised: Yes ☐ (Please describe below)   No ☐

2.22 To what extent do you agree/disagree that:

	Strongly disagree	Disagree	Neutral	Agree	Strongly agree

i. Risk management practices employed in your organisation have delivered benefits that exceed the cost of those practices ☐ ☐ ☐ ☐ ☐

Contact Details

If you have ticked a, b or c, please provide your:

✓

a) You would like to receive a copy of the survey results ☐   Name

b) Can we contact you if we have any follow up questions ☐   organisation

Phone no.

c) Would you be willing to take part in a one-to-one interview to explore risk management further ☐   E-mail

THANK YOU FOR YOUR HELP

Please return the completed questionnaire in the enclosed freepost envelope to: Gary Burke, Finance, Accounting & Law Group, Aston Business School, Aston University, Birmingham B4 7ET, Tel 0121 359 3011 ext 5082. If you have any questions or queries about the questionnaire, please e-mail me at burkegt@aston.ac.uk

Appendix 2

Appendix 2 contains more detailed statistical information in relation to those tables in Chapter 3 which contain only mean and standard deviation data.

T 3.4   Competitive intensity, uncertainty and risk

a) What is the degree of competitive intensity in your industry/sector

	Very low	Low	Medium	High	Very high
Total sample	8.2%	9.7%	23.0%	35.8%	23.3%
CIMA	11.3%	11.3%	23.8%	32.1%	21.7%
FTSE	0.0%	8.2%	22.4%	42.9%	26.5%
SME	0.0%	2.4%	19.5%	48.8%	29.3%

b) What is the degree of uncertainty in your industry/sector environment

	Very low	Low	Medium	High	Very high
Total sample	0.9%	16.7%	33.3%	37.0%	12.1%
CIMA	1.3%	19.6%	31.3%	36.7%	11.3%
FTSE	0.0%	8.2%	36.7%	42.9%	12.2%
SME	0.0%	9.8%	41.5%	31.7%	17.1%

c) What is the degree of risk faced by your organisation

	Very low	Low	Medium	High	Very high
Total sample	0.6%	9.1%	43.5%	37.8%	9.1%
CIMA	0.8%	10.8%	39.2%	40.4%	8.8%
FTSE	0.0%	2.0%	56.0%	28.0%	14.0%
SME	0.0%	7.3%	53.7%	34.1%	4.9%

d) What is the degree of risk faced within your industry/sector

	Very low	Low	Medium	High	Very high
Total sample	0.0%	9.4%	40.5%	41.1%	9.1%
CIMA	0.0%	10.4%	39.0%	42.7%	7.9%
FTSE	0.0%	6.1%	40.8%	38.8%	14.3%
SME	0.0%	7.3%	48.8%	34.1%	9.8%

a) Legislation (including Combined Code) is a driver of risk management in your organisation:

	Strongly disagree	Disagree	Neutral	Agree	Strongly agree
Total sample	0.9%	7.0%	20.4%	55.9%	15.8%
CIMA	0.8%	5.9%	22.3%	54.6%	16.4%
FTSE	2.0%	14.0%	12.0%	54.0%	18.0%
SME	0.0%	4.9%	19.5%	65.9%	9.8%

b) Regulatory bodies drive risk management in the organisation:

	Strongly disagree	Disagree	Neutral	Agree	Strongly agree
Total sample	0.6%	6.4%	24.3%	50.8%	17.9%
CIMA	0.4%	5.9%	24.4%	50.8%	18.5%
FTSE	2.0%	12.0%	20.0%	52.0%	14.0%
SME	0.0%	2.4%	29.3%	48.8%	19.5%

c) Expectations of shareholders/ analysts drive risk management in the organisation:

	Strongly disagree	Disagree	Neutral	Agree	Strongly agree
Total sample	5.5%	12.3%	31.6%	43.3%	7.4%
CIMA	6.0%	14.0%	33.2%	38.7%	8.1%
FTSE	6.0%	4.0%	14.0%	70.0%	6.0%
SME	2.4%	12.2%	43.9%	36.6%	4.9%

d) The competitive business environment drives risk management in the organisation:

	Strongly disagree	Disagree	Neutral	Agree	Strongly agree
Total sample	1.5%	6.1%	21.6%	60.8%	10.0%
CIMA	2.1%	5.4%	22.2%	60.7%	9.6%
FTSE	0.0%	12.0%	24.0%	50.0%	14.0%
SME	0.0%	2.5%	15.0%	75.0%	7.5%

e) Customers/clients who demand it drive risk management in the organisation:

	Strongly disagree	Disagree	Neutral	Agree	Strongly agree
Total sample	1.8%	12.2%	29.6%	46.3%	10.1%
CIMA	0.8%	8.8%	29.8%	47.9%	12.6%
FTSE	8.2%	20.4%	34.7%	36.7%	0.0%
SME	0.0%	22.0%	22.0%	48.8%	7.3%

f) A critical event or near miss was the driver for risk management in the organisation:

	Strongly disagree	Disagree	Neutral	Agree	Strongly agree
Total sample	0.9%	16.1%	27.1%	40.1%	15.8%
CIMA	1.3%	13.4%	27.7%	39.1%	18.5%
FTSE	0.0%	30.0%	26.0%	38.0%	6.0%
SME	0.0%	14.6%	24.4%	48.8%	12.2%

g) Board/top management drive risk management in the organisation:

	Strongly disagree	Disagree	Neutral	Agree	Strongly agree
Total sample	0.0%	3.3%	24.0%	58.1%	14.6%
CIMA	0.0%	3.4%	24.4%	58.8%	13.4%
FTSE	0.0%	4.0%	22.0%	56.0%	18.0%
SME	0.0%	2.4%	24.4%	56.1%	17.1%

T 3.6   Stakeholder involvement in risk management

a) Shareholders /analysts are involved in your organisation's risk management

	Strongly disagree	Disagree	Neutral	Agree	Strongly agree
Total sample	18.7%	32.0%	21.2%	24.1%	4.1%
CIMA	18.9%	33.5%	20.7%	22.5%	4.4%
FTSE	18.8%	25.0%	31.3%	22.9%	2.1%
SME	17.1%	31.7%	12.2%	34.1%	4.9%

b) Suppliers are involved in your organisation's risk management

	Strongly disagree	Disagree	Neutral	Agree	Strongly agree
Total sample	14.3%	33.2%	26.4%	24.8%	1.2%
CIMA	12.1%	35.8%	27.6%	23.3%	1.3%
FTSE	22.4%	20.4%	28.6%	26.5%	2.0%
SME	17.1%	34.1%	17.1%	31.7%	0.0%

c) Customers are involved in your organisation's risk management

	Strongly disagree	Disagree	Neutral	Agree	Strongly agree
Total sample	9.3%	19.2%	21.7%	45.8%	4.0%
CIMA	7.3%	21.9%	20.6%	45.5%	4.7%
FTSE	14.3%	14.3%	30.6%	38.8%	2.0%
SME	14.6%	9.8%	17.1%	56.1%	2.4%

d) Banks/financiers are involved in your organisation's risk management	Strongly disagree	Disagree	Neutral	Agree	Strongly agree
Total sample	10.3%	21.5%	26.5%	37.7%	4.0%
CIMA	9.1%	24.1%	27.6%	33.6%	5.6%
FTSE	14.3%	10.2%	26.5%	49.0%	0.0%
SME	12.5%	20.0%	20.0%	47.5%	0.0%

T 3.7   Propensity to take risks

a) How would you describe your personal propensity to take risks:	Refuse to take risks	Prefer not take risks	Neutral	Willing to take risks	Keen to take risks
Total sample	0.9%	30.3%	23.7%	43.8%	1.2%
CIMA	1.2%	35.5%	24.0%	38.0%	1.2%
FTSE	0.0%	10.0%	26.0%	62.0%	2.0%
SME	0.0%	24.4%	19.5%	56.1%	0.0%

b) How would you describe your organisation's propensity to take risks	Refuse to take risks	Prefer not take risks	Neutral	Willing to take risks	Keen to take risks
Total sample	0.9%	39.4%	17.3%	40.6%	1.8%
CIMA	1.3%	44.4%	16.3%	36.8%	1.3%
FTSE	0.0%	22.0%	20.0%	52.0%	6.0%
SME	0.0%	31.7%	19.5%	48.8%	0.0%

T 3.8   Changing propensity to take risks

a) Over the last two years, has your personal propensity to take risks:	Reduced significantly	Reduced a little	Not changed	Increased a little	Increased significantly
Total sample	2.7%	20.7%	45.9%	28.8%	1.8%
CIMA	2.5%	19.0%	43.0%	33.9%	1.7%
FTSE	2.0%	28.0%	54.0%	14.0%	2.0%
SME	4.9%	22.0%	53.7%	17.1%	2.4%

b) Over the last two years, has your organisation's propensity to take risks:

	Reduced significantly	Reduced a little	Not changed	Increased a little	Increased significantly
Total sample	3.0%	18.4%	44.1%	30.5%	3.9%
CIMA	2.9%	17.1%	41.7%	35.0%	3.3%
FTSE	4.0%	22.0%	58.0%	14.0%	2.0%
SME	2.4%	22.0%	41.5%	24.4%	9.8%

T 3.12 Supporting processes and culture

a) Your organisation has an effective risk management policy

	Strongly disagree	Disagree	Neutral	Agree	Strongly agree
Total sample	1.2%	14.8%	26.1%	48.8%	9.1%
CIMA	1.3%	17.5%	27.9%	44.6%	8.8%
FTSE	2.0%	4.1%	14.3%	65.3%	14.3%
SME	0.0%	12.2%	29.3%	53.7%	4.9%

b) Risks are well understood throughout your organisation

	Strongly disagree	Disagree	Neutral	Agree	Strongly agree
Total sample	2.4%	18.5%	27.3%	48.5%	3.3%
CIMA	3.3%	20.8%	27.5%	44.6%	3.8%
FTSE	0.0%	14.3%	22.4%	61.2%	2.0%
SME	0.0%	9.8%	31.7%	56.1%	2.4%

c) Controlling risk is highly centralised within your organisation

	Strongly disagree	Disagree	Neutral	Agree	Strongly agree
Total sample	4.5%	25.8%	20.6%	42.7%	6.4%
CIMA	2.9%	22.1%	23.8%	43.8%	7.5%
FTSE	14.3%	32.7%	14.3%	36.7%	2.0%
SME	2.4%	39.0%	9.8%	43.9%	4.9%

d) Your organisation regularly reviews internal controls

	Strongly disagree	Disagree	Neutral	Agree	Strongly agree
Total sample	1.2%	9.1%	14.9%	62.0%	12.8%
CIMA	1.7%	10.5%	15.5%	59.4%	13.0%
FTSE	0.0%	0.0%	14.3%	75.5%	10.2%
SME	0.0%	12.2%	12.2%	61.0%	14.6%

e) Risk management is embedded in your organisation's culture

	Strongly disagree	Disagree	Neutral	Agree	Strongly agree
Total sample	4.2%	21.2%	28.8%	39.1%	6.7%
CIMA	4.6%	22.5%	28.3%	37.9%	6.7%
FTSE	4.1%	12.2%	34.7%	40.8%	8.2%
SME	2.4%	24.4%	24.4%	43.9%	4.9%

f) Formal procedures are in place for reporting risks

	Strongly disagree	Disagree	Neutral	Agree	Strongly agree
Total sample	2.4%	15.8%	19.5%	53.2%	9.1%
CIMA	3.3%	17.2%	21.8%	48.5%	9.2%
FTSE	0.0%	8.2%	12.2%	69.4%	10.2%
SME	0.0%	17.1%	14.6%	61.0%	7.3%

g) The level of internal control is appropriate for the risks faced

	Strongly disagree	Disagree	Neutral	Agree	Strongly agree
Total sample	0.9%	15.5%	23.6%	55.8%	4.2%
CIMA	1.3%	17.9%	25.8%	51.7%	3.3%
FTSE	0.0%	8.2%	20.4%	69.4%	2.0%
SME	0.0%	9.8%	14.6%	63.4%	12.2%

h) Your organisation is effective at prioritising risks

	Strongly disagree	Disagree	Neutral	Agree	Strongly agree
Total sample	2.7%	15.8%	36.1%	42.7%	2.7%
CIMA	3.3%	17.9%	38.8%	37.5%	2.5%
FTSE	2.0%	10.2%	30.6%	55.1%	2.0%
SME	0.0%	9.8%	26.8%	58.5%	4.9%

i) Changes to risks are assessed and reported on an ongoing basis

	Strongly disagree	Disagree	Neutral	Agree	Strongly agree
Total sample	2.4%	17.6%	22.2%	52.3%	5.5%
CIMA	2.5%	20.5%	24.7%	48.1%	4.2%
FTSE	4.1%	6.1%	14.3%	67.3%	8.2%
SME	0.0%	14.6%	17.1%	58.5%	9.8%

T 3.14 Usage rate of risk management methods

a) Usage rate of basic methods measure

	Low 1	2	Medium 3	4	High 5
Total sample	5.8%	25.7%	43.7%	21.5%	3.2%
CIMA	8.1%	25.6%	43.5%	20.2%	2.7%
FTSE	0.0%	17.0%	46.8%	29.8%	6.4%
SME	0.0%	36.6%	41.5%	19.5%	2.4%

b) Usage rate of sophisticated methods measure

	Low 1	2	Medium 3	4	High 5
Total sample	37.5%	33.3%	19.9%	5.4%	3.8%
CIMA	31.4%	36.3%	21.1%	6.3%	4.9%
FTSE	53.1%	22.4%	16.3%	6.1%	2.0%
SME	52.5%	30.0%	17.5%	0.0%	0.0%

c) Experience, intuition, hindsight, judgement usage

	Low 1	2	Medium 3	4	High 5
Total sample	1.2%	4.9%	23.7%	44.0%	26.2%
CIMA	0.9%	4.7%	25.1%	45.1%	24.3%
FTSE	2.0%	6.1%	22.4%	36.7%	32.7%
SME	2.4%	4.9%	17.1%	46.3%	29.3%

d) Use of auditors or external consultants usage

	Low 1	2	Medium 3	4	High 5
Total sample	18.0%	17.4%	29.5%	25.8%	9.3%
CIMA	17.2%	17.7%	25.9%	27.2%	12.1%
FTSE	18.4%	18.4%	46.9%	14.3%	2.0%
SME	22.0%	14.6%	29.3%	31.7%	2.4%

T 3.16 Organisation's management accounting and RM functions are integrated

a) Organisation's accounting and risk management functions are integrated

	Strongly disagree	Disagree	Neutral	Agree	Strongly agree
Total sample	6.7%	35.7%	30.3%	24.8%	2.5%
CIMA	6.7%	35.7%	30.3%	24.8%	2.5%

a) To what degree has risk management improved performance and or outcomes in: Corporate planning

	No improvement 1	2	Some improvement 3	4	Significant improvement 5
Total sample	9.6%	20.1%	47.9%	20.8%	1.6%
CIMA	10.8%	22.0%	46.6%	19.3%	1.3%
FTSE	6.0%	12.0%	56.0%	24.0%	2.0%
SME	7.5%	20.0%	45.0%	25.0%	2.5%

b) Improved resource allocation and utilisation

	No improvement 1	2	Some improvement 3	4	Significant improvement 5
Total sample	9.7%	24.1%	42.3%	21.3%	2.5%
CIMA	10.5%	24.0%	41.0%	22.7%	1.7%
FTSE	8.0%	28.0%	40.0%	20.0%	4.0%
SME	7.5%	20.0%	52.5%	15.0%	5.0%

c) Improved management reporting

	No improvement 1	2	Some improvement 3	4	Significant improvement 5
Total sample	9.1%	16.9%	39.2%	29.2%	5.6%
CIMA	10.5%	19.2%	40.2%	25.8%	4.4%
FTSE	8.0%	12.0%	40.0%	30.0%	10.0%
SME	2.5%	10.0%	32.5%	47.5%	7.5%

d) Improved communication within the organisation

	No improvement 1	2	Some improvement 3	4	Significant improvement 5
Total sample	13.2%	24.5%	37.1%	22.6%	2.5%
CIMA	14.0%	27.9%	35.8%	20.5%	1.7%
FTSE	14.3%	22.4%	40.8%	20.4%	2.0%
SME	7.5%	7.5%	40.0%	37.5%	7.5%

e) Improved relationships with shareholders

	No improvement 1	2	Some improvement 3	4	Significant improvement 5
Total sample	27.5%	28.5%	28.5%	13.7%	1.8%
CIMA	27.1%	27.6%	29.6%	13.6%	2.0%
FTSE	31.9%	23.4%	25.5%	19.1%	0.0%
SME	23.7%	39.5%	26.3%	7.9%	2.6%

f) Improved relationships with customers/clients	No improvement 1	2	Some improvement 3	4	Significant improvement 5
Total sample	14.3%	25.5%	38.2%	19.7%	2.2%
CIMA	14.3%	25.4%	38.4%	20.1%	1.8%
FTSE	20.0%	30.0%	34.0%	12.0%	4.0%
SME	7.5%	20.0%	42.5%	27.5%	2.5%

g) Improved relationships with suppliers	No improvement 1	2	Some improvement 3	4	Significant improvement 5
Total sample	22.5%	27.0%	35.6%	14.0%	1.0%
CIMA	22.7%	24.4%	38.7%	12.9%	1.3%
FTSE	30.0%	30.0%	24.0%	16.0%	0.0%
SME	12.5%	37.5%	32.5%	17.5%	0.0%

h) Improved management of organisational change	No improvement 1	2	Some improvement 3	4	Significant improvement 5
Total sample	9.7%	21.9%	38.2%	27.6%	2.5%
CIMA	11.4%	23.6%	37.6%	25.3%	2.2%
FTSE	8.0%	22.0%	34.0%	34.0%	2.0%
SME	2.5%	12.5%	47.5%	32.5%	5.0%

i) Improved reputation	No improvement 1	2	Some improvement 3	4	Significant improvement 5
Total sample	12.3%	20.5%	35.0%	27.4%	4.7%
CIMA	12.3%	22.9%	34.8%	26.0%	4.0%
FTSE	16.0%	18.0%	38.0%	24.0%	4.0%
SME	7.5%	10.0%	32.5%	40.0%	10.0%

j) Improved recognition and uptake of opportunities	No improvement 1	2	Some improvement 3	4	Significant improvement 5
Total sample	11.1%	22.5%	37.0%	26.3%	3.2%
CIMA	10.6%	23.9%	38.5%	24.3%	2.7%
FTSE	16.0%	20.0%	34.0%	26.0%	4.0%
SME	7.5%	17.5%	32.5%	37.5%	5.0%

k) Improved employee confidence in carrying out their duties	No improvement 1	2	Some improvement 3	4	Significant improvement 5
Total sample	13.1%	27.8%	37.5%	20.0%	1.6%
CIMA	14.3%	30.4%	33.9%	19.6%	1.7%
FTSE	12.0%	24.0%	52.0%	12.0%	0.0%
SME	7.5%	17.5%	40.0%	32.5%	2.5%

l) Are there any other improvements or benefits that have been realised

	Yes	No
Total sample	9.5%	90.5%
CIMA	5.8%	94.2%
FTSE	28.6%	71.4%
SME	8.7%	91.3%

m) RM practices employed in your organisation have delivered benefits that exceed the cost of those practices

	Strongly disagree	Disagree	Neutral	Agree	Strongly agree
Total sample	2.1%	7.6%	39.8%	44.1%	6.4%
CIMA	2.1%	8.8%	41.0%	42.7%	5.4%
FTSE	4.0%	6.0%	32.0%	46.0%	12.0%
SME	0.0%	2.5%	42.5%	50.0%	5.0%

T 3.19 Risk management options employed

a) Transferring the risk using insurance, hedging, contracts, joint ventures or partnerships, etc

	Low 1	2	Medium 3	4	High 5
Total sample	16.4%	11.9%	30.4%	28.9%	12.5%
CIMA	19.7%	12.2%	31.1%	24.4%	12.6%
FTSE	4.0%	8.0%	26.0%	42.0%	20.0%
SME	12.0%	14.6%	31.7%	39.0%	2.4%

b) Decreasing the likelihood of the risk through management action e.g.quality management, project management, R&D, training, etc.

	Low 1	2	Medium 3	4	High 5
Total sample	2.4%	8.8%	29.1%	44.5%	15.2%
CIMA	3.3%	9.6%	32.2%	40.6%	14.2%
FTSE	0.0%	4.0%	22.0%	54.0%	20.0%
SME	0.0%	9.8%	19.5%	56.1%	14.6%

c) Decreasing adverse consequences of the risk using contingency, business continuity, fraud control plans, etc.

	Low 1	2	Medium 3	4	High 5
Total sample	5.8%	16.7%	32.8%	36.5%	8.2%
CIMA	7.1%	18.1%	31.9%	33.2%	9.7%
FTSE	2.0%	10.0%	36.0%	44.0%	8.0%
SME	2.4%	17.1%	34.1%	46.3%	0.0%

T 3.20   Perceived effectiveness of risk management approaches

a) Effectiveness of transferring the risk using insurance etc.

	Low 1	2	Medium 3	4	High 5
Total sample	15.4%	13.5%	29.2%	31.1%	10.8%
CIMA	19.5%	10.6%	29.7%	30.5%	9.7%
FTSE	0.0%	28.6%	18.4%	32.7%	20.4%
SME	10.0%	12.5%	40.0%	32.5%	5.0%

b) Effectiveness of decreasing the likelihood of the risk through management action etc.

	Low 1	2	Medium 3	4	High 5
Total sample	3.4%	8.6%	37.0%	38.5%	12.5%
CIMA	3.8%	9.3%	39.7%	37.1%	10.1%
FTSE	2.0%	2.0%	28.0%	46.0%	22.0%
SME	2.5%	12.5%	32.5%	37.5%	15.0%

c) Effectiveness of decreasing adverse consequences of the risk using contingency etc.

	Low 1	2	Medium 3	4	High 5
Total sample	7.4%	16.0%	39.1%	29.8%	7.7%
CIMA	8.1%	18.7%	37.0%	28.5%	7.7%
FTSE	4.0%	6.0%	44.0%	36.0%	10.0%
SME	7.5%	12.5%	45.0%	30.0%	5.0%

d) Relationship between personal propensity to take risk and the organization's propensity to take risk

Total sample	0.332**
CIMA	0.210**
FTSE	0.460**
SME	0.702**

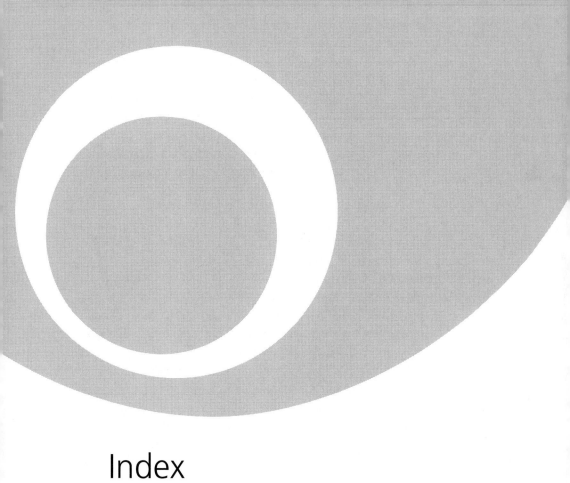

Index

Index